Materials Science
DYES, PAINTS, AND ADHESIVES

making use of the secrets of matter

First published in 2003 by
Atlantic Europe Publishing Company Ltd.

Copyright © 2003
Atlantic Europe Publishing Company Ltd.

Reprinted in 2005

All rights reserved. No part of this publication may be reproduced, stored in a retrieval system, or transmitted in any form or by any means—electronic, mechanical, photocopying, recording, or otherwise—without prior permission of the publisher.

Author
Brian Knapp, BSc, PhD

Art Director
Duncan McCrae, BSc

Senior Designer
Adele Humphries, BA, PGCE

Editors
Mary Sanders, BSc, and Gillian Gatehouse

Illustrations
David Woodroffe

Design and production
EARTHSCAPE EDITIONS

Scanning and retouching
Global Graphics sro, Czech Republic

Print
WKT Company Ltd., China

Materials Science – Volume 6: Dyes, paints, and adhesives
A CIP record for this book is available from the British Library

ISBN 1 86214 320 X

Acknowledgments
The publishers would like to thank the following for their kind help and advice: *Susan J. Beates*; *Jack Brettle*; *Brother Industries Ltd (Japan)*; *The Drake Well Museum, Commonwealth of Pennsylvania Historical and Museum Commission* for the oil samples page 16; *Gordon Jones*; *Wing King Tong Co., Ltd*; *Barbara T. Zolli*.

Picture credits
All photographs are from the Earthscape Editions photolibrary except the following: (c=center t=top b=bottom l=left r=right)

Brother Industries Ltd (Japan) COVER background, 40b.

This product is manufactured from sustainable managed forests. For every tree cut down, at least one more is planted.

Contents

1: Dyes and pigments   4
  Color mixing   4
  Coloring materials   6
  How dyes work   6
  Kinds of dyes   7
  Pigments   8
  Making synthetic dyes   10
  Mordants   10

2: The history of making coloring materials   11
  The science of making color: the first step   14
  New advances   15
  The developing use of crude oil   16

3: Making and using dyes   17
  The nature of materials   17
  Getting a deep color   18
  Making the dye hold fast   20
  Vat dyeing   20
  Disperse dyeing   21
  Ingrain dyeing   22
  Dyes used as fabric and paper brighteners   24
  Dyes as food colorings   25

4: Paints, varnishes, and other protective coatings   27
  Paints   27
  Preparation coats   30
  Antirust paint   33
  Modern paints and protective coatings   34
  Preservatives   36
  Reflective paints   39
  Powder coatings   40

5: Adhesives   41
  The history of adhesives   42
  Making adhesives work   43
  How adhesives work   45
  "Wetting" the surfaces   46
  Applying adhesives sparingly   47
  Natural adhesives   48
  Synthetic adhesives   50
  How common adhesives are used   50

Set glossary   58

Set index   65

(*Left*) Washing powder with small granules of blue dye intended to give the impression of a whiter wash.

1: Dyes and pigments

When you look at an object, the chances are that you think about its shape, size, and weight, and hardly notice the surface at all. But it is the surface coatings that give many materials some important properties. For example, without colored surface materials the goods we make would look far more dull and uninteresting, or they might corrode or easily become dirty.

Paints and other materials that we apply to surfaces to make them more durable or more attractive are examples of *surface* materials. But we use some surface materials in a quite different way—to hold things together. Surface materials of this kind are called ADHESIVES. Without them we would be forced to bolt, tie, or nail everything together—as people did in the past.

This, then, is a book about the wide variety of surface materials that we use

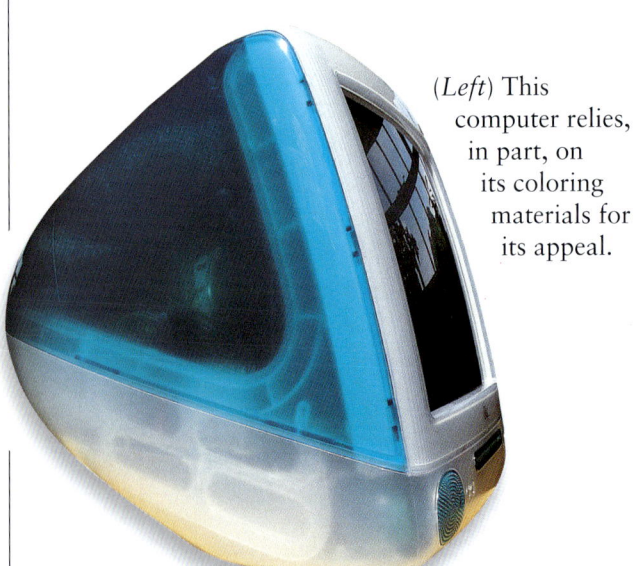

(*Left*) This computer relies, in part, on its coloring materials for its appeal.

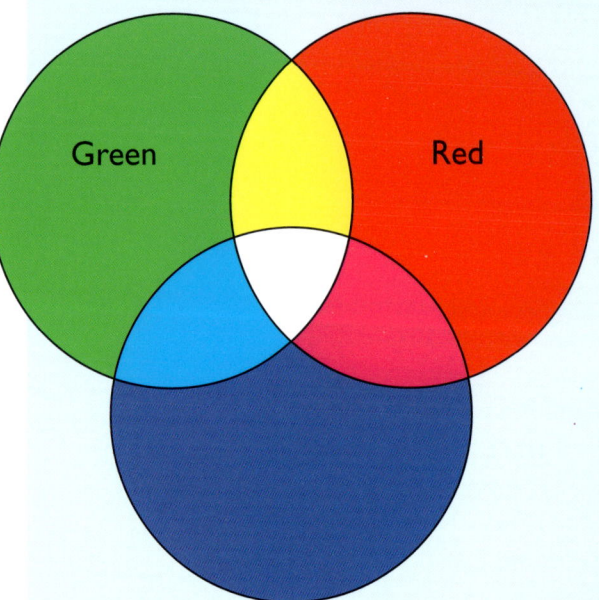

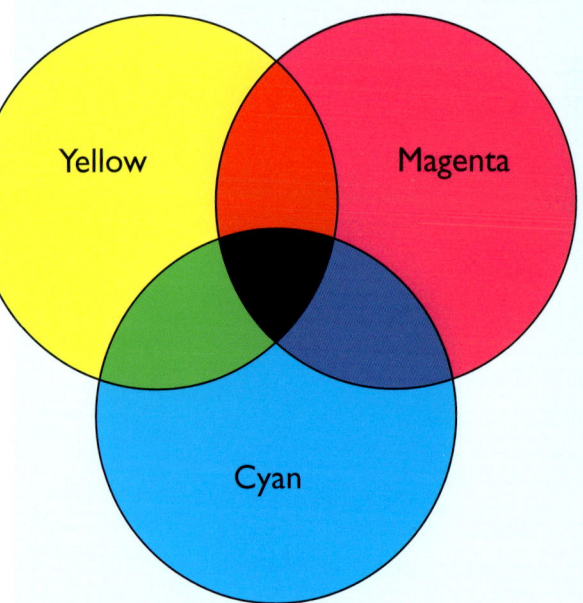

Color mixing. The two ways of mixing colors are additive (*above*) and subtractive (*below*).

Color mixing

The eye can distinguish ten million colors. However, there are only three PRIMARY COLORS from which all other colors can be made. For light rays sent from a source of light (transmitted colors) they are red, green, and blue. These are the colors used to make a color television picture, for example.

When light is sent directly to the eye, the primary colors appear to add together. Red and green make yellow. Green and blue produce cyan. Blue and red make magenta. Red, green, and blue produce white.

However, when light reflected from the world around us reaches the eye, the primary colors are different. The primaries become magenta (bluish-red), yellow, and cyan (blue-green).

These *reflected* primary colors absorb some of the white light that reaches them and filter out, or subtract, certain light waves. These primaries are the opposite (called complementary) colors from the red, green, and blue primaries. For example, a magenta filter will take out the green part of the light, while a yellow filter takes out the blue, and cyan takes out the red. If you put a magenta filter over a yellow filter and then added a cyan filter, or if you added magenta to yellow or cyan, no light would leave at all. That is how the black color of paint is created.

All colors are produced by mixing colors in one of two ways: by adding or by subtracting. To get color mixtures by adding, new sources of light are added.

Mixing colors for use on surfaces is the opposite of transmitting light. In this case the idea is to take certain colors out of white light so that only the desired color is reflected from the surface. That is why mixing paints is called subtractive mixing. All paints, inks, and dyes work this way. For example, mixing yellow and blue pigments causes the absorption of all colors but green.

The colors for subtraction are those that absorb red, green, and blue light. They are blue-green (cyan), red-blue (magenta), and yellow. Confusion arises when some people call the primary colors used in paints and dyes red, yellow, and blue (instead of magenta, yellow, and cyan). For paints and dyes it is always best to think of the colors as red-absorbing, green-absorbing, and blue-absorbing. Then you can see that transmitted and reflected light are part of the same system.

(*Below*) The way this house is painted makes it much more attractive and also preserves the surface from the weather.

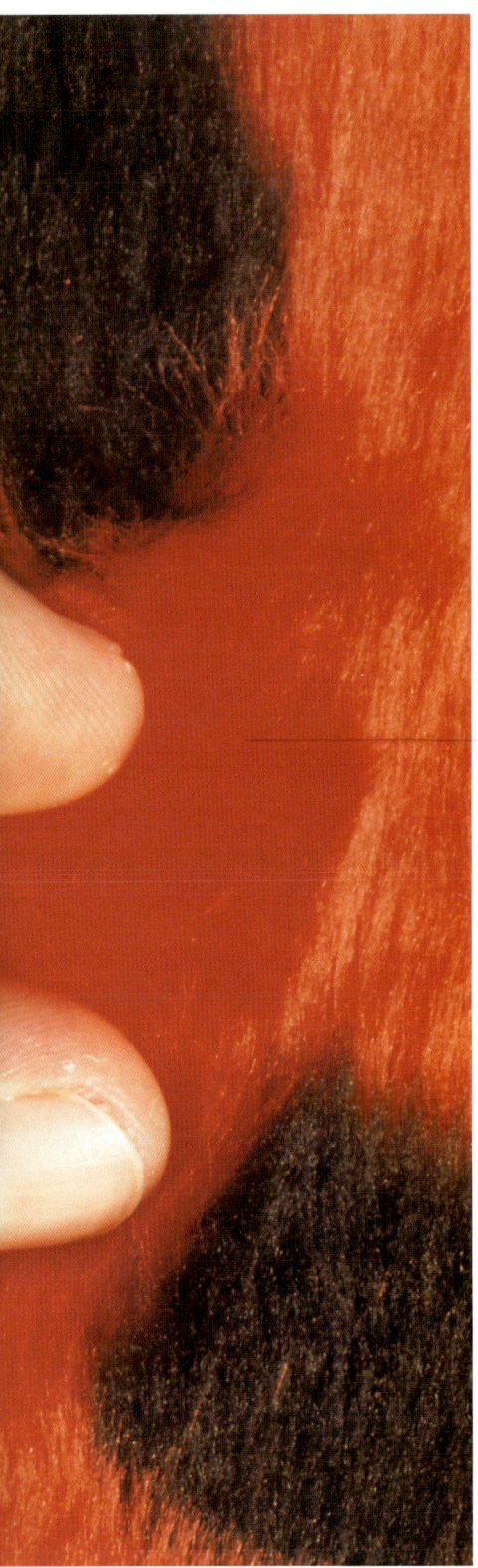

(*Above*) Dyed fibers give a wonderful variety to the clothes we wear.

everywhere and the way they help add more variety and usefulness to the things around us. We will be looking at dyes and pigments in the first part of the book and adhesives toward the end.

Coloring materials

We see the world in color. Nature has produced an almost infinite variety of colors in its plants, animals, rocks, and minerals. We find color pleasing. It also gives us vital information, such as warning of danger. To make things colored, we use two types of colored chemicals: DYES and PIGMENTS.

A dye, such as used in dyes for textiles or in food colorings, is a SOLUTION containing a colored substance DISSOLVED in it. During dyeing, dye MOLECULES have to be deposited from the solution onto the material that is being dyed. This has to happen in a way that makes them INSOLUBLE and not likely to return to the solution again.

A pigment (such as is used in paints) is a colored insoluble substance (for example, a powder) SUSPENDED in a liquid. It does not form a solution.

Both dyes and pigments are also known as COLORANTS (color-making substances). The colorant may be added to a cold liquid, or it may be added to a hot liquid, for example, a plastic while it is being made.

How dyes work

We see objects in color because they absorb all of the parts (WAVELENGTHS) of white light except the color we see.

All materials absorb some light. Black objects absorb all visible light; white objects reflect all visible light. Only special materials absorb selectively parts of the visible light and so can be dyes or pigments.

Every color we see is produced by light rays of a particular range of wavelengths. The narrower the range of wavelengths, the less "contaminated" the color is by nearby colors, and so the more brilliant it appears.

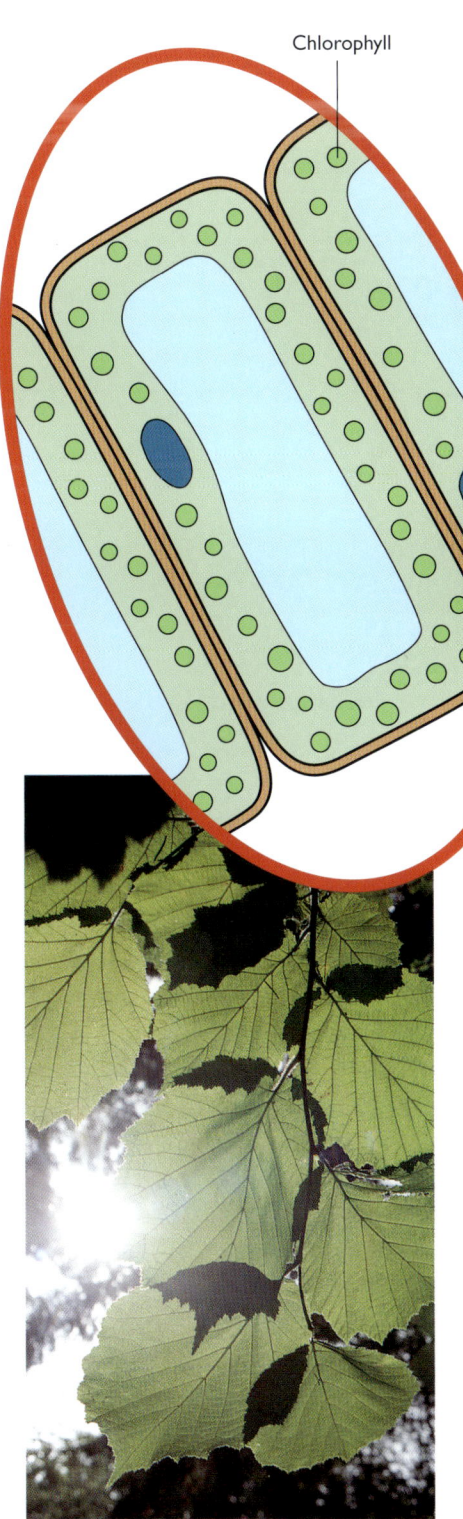

(Below) The green color in plants is produced by tiny particles of chlorophyll inside the cells. Synthetic dyes have to copy the light-absorbing nature of natural substances like this.

Chlorophyll

ARTIFICIAL DYES and pigments can be tailored to reflect a very narrow range of light waves. That is why they are more brilliant than NATURAL DYES and pigments. Some people think, however, that this makes artificial dyes look crude, while natural dyes seem richer to them. There is no scientific rationale for this; it is all a matter of taste.

Kinds of dyes

Amazingly, considering there is such a wide variety of color in our world, we make most of our dyes from black materials—coal tar or CRUDE OIL.

The most important market for dyes is in dyeing textiles. Natural fibers, such as wool and cotton, and some artificial fibers, are dyed. Leather, paper, food, and cosmetics also contain dyes.

Until quite recently dyes were extracted from natural substances, mainly plants.

Artificial dyes—which can generally also be called SYNTHETIC DYES because they are synthesized, or made, from basic molecules, not naturally occurring chemicals—were developed starting in 1856. The date is precise because the first artificial dye was made in a chemistry laboratory. In that year William Henry Perkin, an English chemist, discovered the dye known simply as mauve.

Synthetic dyes are often made using ammonia, coal tar, and oil.

Although the first dyes were copies of natural dyes, many modern dyes have no counterpart in nature at all.

Most natural dyes do not stick easily to textiles. As a result, another chemical, called a MORDANT (see page 10), is needed to make the dye bond fast. Most synthetic dyes do not need the use of a mordant. As a result, dyeing with synthetics is faster, easier, and cheaper.

Most synthetic dyes are known as AZO dyes. The name comes from the fact that they are based on a chemical called azobenzene found in both coal tar and crude oil. These new dyes are often more COLORFAST in light than natural dyes are and can be made brighter, more intense, and varied to meet the needs of the customer.

Pigments

A pigment is any substance that has a very intense color, and that is used to color other materials. Synthetic textiles, such as those made from nylon, are often colored by adding pigments during manufacture. That is, in part, because it is very difficult to make a dye hold onto the shiny surface of some plastic textiles.

(*Above and below*) Bright, synthetic printing inks being added to a printing press.

Pigments, rather than dyes, are also used in printing inks, paints, and rubber.

Pigments are not soluble and are held as tiny particles of solid suspended in a liquid. In nature such pigments are found in cells: in skin, hair, scales, and so on. When produced artificially, the pigments are made from ground-up solids and are used to color paint and ink.

Pigments can be made from ORGANIC (carbon-containing substances) or from INORGANIC materials (rock). Organic pigments tend to be more subtle than inorganic ones. Inorganic pigments and synthetic organic pigments are brighter and more LIGHTFAST than natural organic pigments.

For thousands of years most pigments made to color paints were made from natural materials, but the development of synthetic pigments since the 1880s has reversed this, so that now most pigments are synthetic.

Pigments include colors, black, and white. White pigments are used to make other colors lighter. The most commonly used white pigment in paint is titanium dioxide. Other white pigments include calcium carbonate (chalk) and calcium sulfate (plaster), crushed rocks containing skeletons of microscopic diatoms, and china clay (in paper and drugs). Many pigments perform the dual role of a colorant and a FILLER, bulking up a material. That is the case with the use of china clay to whiten and also bulk up fine paper.

Most black pigments are made of carbon. The most common is carbon black made of soot and used in photocopiers, printing machines, and in printing ink.

Colored pigments may be made from minerals. For example, ochers (yellow-browns), siennas (orange-browns), and umbers (browns) are made from iron oxide rocks.

Chromium compounds are used to make yellow, orange, and green pigments. Cadmium

(*Above*) Natural organic pigments are often more subtle than synthetic pigments, as can be seen here in this butterfly.

See **Vol. 3: Wood and paper** *for more on china clay and fine paper.*

(*Below*) White paint, still the most common colored pigment used.

compounds produce brilliant yellow, orange, and red pigments. Copper pigments are brilliant blues and greens.

Azo pigments are the main organic pigments. They produce red, orange, and yellow colors.

Fluorescent pigments are fluorescent dyes that have been made insoluble by chemical reactions.

Making synthetic dyes

As mentioned earlier, most synthetic colorants are made starting with coal tar or crude oil. Coal tar is obtained by heating up coal (without letting it catch fire) until liquids and gases are released from it. Coal tar is one of the liquids. Crude oil begins as a liquid and so is simpler to use.

Coal tar and crude oil are mixtures of chemicals and do not directly make dyes. To make dyes, the ingredients needed, such as benzene, have to be separated from the other chemicals in the mixture. That is done by DISTILLATION—heating the liquids in a controlled way until the components of the mixture boil off one by one. The gases are then collected separately and turned back into liquids.

Raw materials (called feedstock) for dyes are not needed in the vast quantities that, say, car gas is. As a result, a continuous production line is not used, and dyes are made in batches as and when needed.

Mordants

A mordant (from the Latin word for "to bite") is a chemical that is used with a dye to make it stick. It is a sort of molecular glue. The mordant is a chemical that readily sticks to molecules on the surface of the textile or other material to be dyed. It also attracts molecules of dye from the solution and holds them fast.

Alum (potassium aluminum sulfate) is the main mordant and is found in many clay rocks. Compounds of iron, copper, and tin have all also traditionally been used as mordants.

(Below) This is alum in crystalline form.

(Below) In this laboratory experiment a nearly colorless suspension of aluminum hydroxide is added to a purple vegetable dye and thoroughly shaken.

Soon a precipitate with the dye stuck to its surface settles, leaving only a colorless liquid above. This clearly shows that the aluminum hydroxide, which has been formed from alum, is an effective mordant.

2: The history of making coloring materials

Nature is filled with color. Since earliest times people have tried to make and use color. All colors are made of chemical compounds, so the history of color is closely tied to the understanding of how the colors can be made.

With no chemical understanding to help them develop their own colors, people in early times naturally turned to trying to use the coloring substances in plants and rocks.

Cave paintings from over 28,000 years ago contain colors made using soot from burning wood or by using pieces of soft colored stone, such as chalk or iron-rich sandstone.

However, over the centuries plants proved to be a better and more flexible source of color, so that by the time of the first civilizations, most of the dyes and pigments were made from drying, boiling, or fermenting plants.

Egyptian tombs contain both wall paintings and fabrics that use dyes and pigments. Inscriptions found in ancient Egypt show that over 4,000 years ago, the dyeing industry was so well established that it was possible to write down methods for dyeing.

Making natural dyes proved a time-consuming and difficult business. Indigo, for example, was fermented in vats. It released a colorless solution. The clothes were steeped in it and then exposed to the air. Only as the dye dried did the chemical absorbed onto the cloth react with the oxygen in the air to produce a blue color.

(Below) Roots, leaves, flowers, and the other parts of plants make a wide range of colors that can be used as dyes.

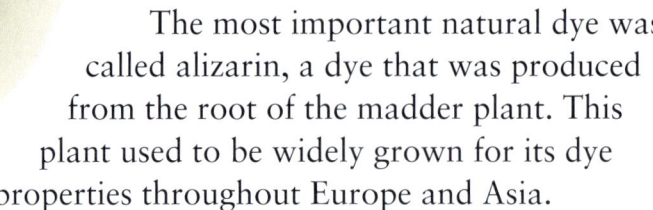

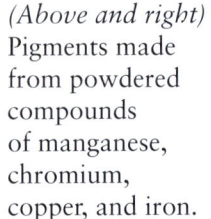

(Above and right) Pigments made from powdered compounds of manganese, chromium, copper, and iron.

The most important natural dye was called alizarin, a dye that was produced from the root of the madder plant. This plant used to be widely grown for its dye properties throughout Europe and Asia.

The color you could get from the madder plant depended on the mordant used. If aluminum compounds were used, the dye produced a red color; if iron compounds were used, the color made was deep purple; and if mixtures of aluminum and iron compounds were used, the color produced was between red and purple.

When dyes were extracted from plants, it was not possible to make one batch of dye exactly the same as the next. Every dye was therefore unique in shade, or color intensity. The best dyers were those who had the skill to blend the ingredients to get the subtle colors that wealthy people wanted. As a result, the production of dyes was a profitable business, and master dyers went to great trouble to hide their secret formulas.

The dyes that could be made still depended on the plants that could be obtained by trade. Thus, soon after the New World was linked to Europe in 1492, a new range of plants was discovered that could be used for dyes. Dyes obtained from brazilwood, for example, produced a new type of red color when used with aluminum as a mordant, a brown when iron was used, and a pink when combined with tin mordants.

Logwood, another New World plant, produced a good black when used with a chromium-based mordant.

Other dyes came from insects. For example, a scarlet color was produced from the crushed bodies of Mexican insects called *Coccus cacti*. It was cochineal, and it produced a scarlet colored dye called carmine. It became the standard dye for producing scarlet British uniforms, and until 1954 the color was fixed using a tin oxide mordant.

(Above and below) Lead oxides make a variety of colors. Massicot is a yellow form of lead monoxide. Lead monoxide is one of the most widely used and commercially important metallic compounds. The bright orange-red powder is known as "red lead," while the darkest powder is lead dioxide.

(Left, above, and right) This simple laboratory demonstration shows how dyes can be extracted from natural materials such as plants. Here beet leaves are crushed and then diluted with a liquid in which they will dissolve (in this case acetone). The liquid portion is then passed through a separation column of aluminum oxide and the color components separated. In this case the first green portion is chlorophyll, and the second yellow portion is xanthophyll.

(Below) Some natural dyes and their sources.

Color	Name	Source
Yellow	Saffron	Dried petals of saffron flower
Red	Carmine/cochineal Alizarin	Insects (*Coccus cacti*) Roots of the madder plant
Blue	Indigo, woad	Leaves of the indigo plant
Purple	Tyrian purple	Sea snails (*Murex brandaris*)

Indigo

Xanthophyll

(Left) Natural dyes are still dried and sold in powdered form as in this North African bazaar.

(*Right*) The wool in this traditional tribal weaving is colored using natural dyes. The red is either alizarin (from madder plant) or carmine (from the cochineal insects). Today weavers use synthetic dyes instead.

The science of making color: the first step

The trade of dyeing changed little for thousands of years. Plant extracts provided a range of colors, while pigments came from a variety of rocks.

But it was only as chemistry advanced and synthetic dyes were manufactured that real progress was made to create a new range of dyes.

The sea change in the production of dyes and pigments began in 1856. William Perkin, a chemist, was experimenting with quinine—a substance used to cure malaria. During his experiments he got a blue-colored substance that soaked right into most materials without a mordant. It was called aniline mauve, which became known as "mauve." It was the first dye ever made by chemical reaction as opposed to simply using directly the colored chemicals that were boiled out of plants.

The discovery and manufacture of mauve had the most enormous implications for the dyeing industry. Until this time huge areas of land were used to grow plants that produced natural dyes. But after Perkin's discovery that better

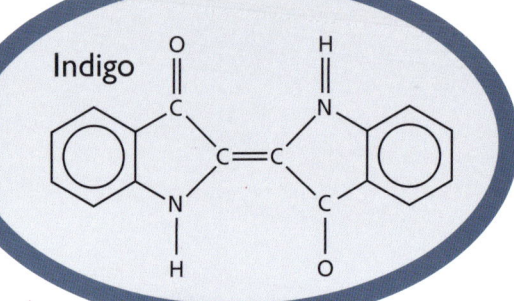

(*Right*) Aniline is a carbon-based chemical used to make dyes. It was first produced by distilling indigo from the indigo plant. This plant is called *Indigofera anil*, and the dye within it has the formula $C_6H_5NH_2$. Notice that it contains both a carbon-based component and a nitrogen-based component. Aniline is now made by reacting ammonia with a form of benzene.

dyes could be made more reliably and cheaply using chemistry, the natural dye industry immediately began to decline, while the synthetic dye industry boomed.

More experiments quickly produced dyes that were better than mauve. Soon it was possible to produce synthetic indigo (the color used to dye blue jeans, synthesized by Adolph von Baeyer in 1880).

New advances

The development of the synthetic dye industry was entirely due to coal tar, but its use was largely accidental at first.

Coal tar was produced in huge quantities as a by-product of making gas from coal. But nobody had any idea what to do with it. It could be used as a waterproofing and even to hold the gravel in road surfaces together, but the amount being produced was getting out of hand.

Chemists then started to find out what was in coal tar by boiling it and collecting separate parts of the mixture by distillation.

The research was led by August Wilhelm von Hofmann, who was the director of the Royal College of Chemistry in England. It was in his laboratory that Perkin discovered mauve. But progress was still mainly by trial and error.

Dissatisfied with this way of working, Hofmann moved to Germany, determined to find the science behind dyeing. It was his move that was to make Germany the world's leading producer of dyes.

During this time it was discovered that most natural plant dyes had in common a ring of atoms (called a benzene ring). Once this was known, it was much easier to plan how to develop this pattern to make new synthetic dyes.

The structure of a typical synthetic yellow

Benzene ring

The structure of a typical synthetic orange

Benzene ring

The structure of a typical synthetic blue

Benzene ring

(Above) It is easy to see how these three dyes are similar.

The developing use of crude oil

The synthetic dye industry was based exclusively on coal tar for about 50 years.

Most of the main dyes were discovered during this period in Germany, and so Germany became the dominant producer of dyes. When World War I approached, the United States and the UK had to look for alternative supplies, and they began to produce dyes from crude oil rather than coal tar.

(Right and below) Crude oil and some of its distillates.

3: Making and using dyes

Dyeing is not simply a matter of swirling a material around in a vat of dye. If this were done, the chances are that when the material was taken out of the vat, it would have taken up no color at all or be streaks and blotches.

The purpose of the dyeing process is to make sure that dyes spread out over the material evenly and that a good layer of dye molecules becomes held fast. If that can be accomplished, the dye will be an intense, even color that will resist being rubbed or washed off, and that will stand up well in the light without fading.

To achieve this, not only do chemical reactions have to take place, but the material must be handled in such a way that it is evenly exposed to the dye.

The nature of materials

The first step in understanding dyeing is to know the microscopic nature of the materials that are to be dyed. Most of them are fibers.

Fibers are long chains of molecules (polymers). For example, wool, silk, and leather are proteins made of units of amino acids. Along these chains are pores where the dye can be held.

Every fiber has its own unique surface. Some fibers are very smooth, some have holes, and some do not. Most natural fibers contain millions of pores. The presence of pores dramatically increases the surface area of the fiber for dyeing. Just 1 kilogram of natural fiber has a surface area (including the surfaces of all pores) of about 45,000 square meters. Synthetic fibers, however, have little surface porosity.

(Below) Every part of every fiber of this felt has been dyed an even green. That is what we expect, but doing so is not as easy as might at first be thought.

See **Vol. 1: Plastics** and **Vol. 7: Fibers** for more on polymers.

Getting a deep color

If too little dye sticks onto the surface of the material, the dye will look weak and may vary in intensity. On the other hand, too much dye wastes material and may also lead to the surface of the dye rubbing away. The ideal thickness for good color and resistance to being worn away is 1,000 to 10,000 dye molecules.

It is much easier to get this layer of molecules onto a natural fiber because of the huge number of surface pores. It is easy for dye molecules to build up in such pores. Indeed, the pores attract and hold the dye.

(*Left*) Natural fibers being dyed and then hung up to dry in Morocco. Even in parts of the world where traditional materials are made, most of the dyes are synthetic.

(Above and right) Tie dyeing illustrates the way that dyes can only reach areas that are fully exposed to a dye.

In tie dyeing, knots are made in the material to prevent the dye reaching them. Various knots are made in different ways as the material is dipped in different colored dyes.

(Left) Batik is another, and much more sophisticated, method of preventing dyes from reaching the material. In this case patterns of wax are used to stop the entry of dyes.

Making the dye hold fast

There are several different kinds of holding force. The strongest are those that involve a chemical reaction. But there are several forces of electrical attraction, too. Often they are good enough.

For example, if the fiber has an electrical charge, then a dye of opposite charge can be used. The fiber will then attract the dye, and the dye will hold fast.

That is how mordants work, too. A mordant binds to a fiber with its molecules lined up in such a way as to leave a surface electrical charge. Parts of the dye molecule are then attracted to these points of electrical charge.

There is another kind of electrical bond involving the hydrogen atoms of one compound and the oxygen atoms of another. It is called hydrogen bonding. To understand how well this attraction works, note that water is made up only of hydrogen atoms attracted to oxygen atoms.

Interestingly, natural fibers that have no pores and are very smooth, such as cellulose, make it possible for some kinds of dye molecules to get very close to the fiber, allowing a strong attraction. This does not work with some synthetic fibers, such as acrylics, however.

Vat dyeing

The most ancient form of dyeing is to dip a fabric into a large container, or vat, filled with dye. This was all done outside and often over a large fire to make the dye hot. It is the basis of what is still called vat dyeing.

Remember that the dye in the vat is in solution, but to stick to the fabric, it must become insoluble, that is, the dye molecules must be attracted out of the liquid and onto the surface of the fiber.

For thousands of years people have used indigo. Indigo is actually insoluble. It has to be altered to a soluble form. The soluble form (called leukoindigo) is colorless, so it may appear as though no dyeing is taking place at all.

(Above) Viscose thread dyed by the disperse dyeing process.

(Below) Nylon thread dyed by the disperse dyeing process.

The dyeing is done in a bath of hot dye. When the dye is hot, not only is the dye more soluble and the dye less viscous (more runny), but the textile is also more wettable because the pores open up. As a result, it is much easier for dye molecules to get in to the textile.

But when leukoindigo is left to dry in air, a reaction occurs between the air and the leukoindigo that makes the dye insoluble again—and it is at this time that the dye becomes visible and blue.

Solid clumps of indigo form as a PRECIPITATE. When they form inside the pores, they are too big to get out. The surplus washes off—which is why the instructions with indigo-dyed clothes (and some others) suggest that the first time they are washed, they are done on their own. As the washing removes excess dye, the color also lightens, producing a more worn look.

Disperse dyeing

Vat dyeing occurs in hot water baths in which the dye is dissolved. Although most natural fibers do attract water, most synthetic ones do not. As a result, vat dyeing is not a successful technique for synthetic fibers.

To get a dye to take on these materials, the dye has to be broken down so that it is made of tiny particles scattered through the solution. The dye has to transfer to the fiber directly, without being dissolved. That is the only way fiber acetate, PET, acrylic, or polyester can be dyed. Because of the large amount of synthetic fiber now being used, this form of dyeing, called disperse dyeing, is one of the most important.

To get the solid pieces of dye into the fiber, the fiber is heated well above the boiling point of water and also put under pressure. Under these conditions the tightly packed structures that make up the synthetic fibers relax and open up a bit, allowing the dye particles to get inside. As the temperature is reduced, the fiber closes up again and so traps the dye particles.

(Above) Disperse, or ingrain, dyeing produces a thread that can be woven into a garment with color all the way through.

See **Vol. 1: Plastics** and **Vol. 7: Fibers** for more on dyeing plastics and fibers.

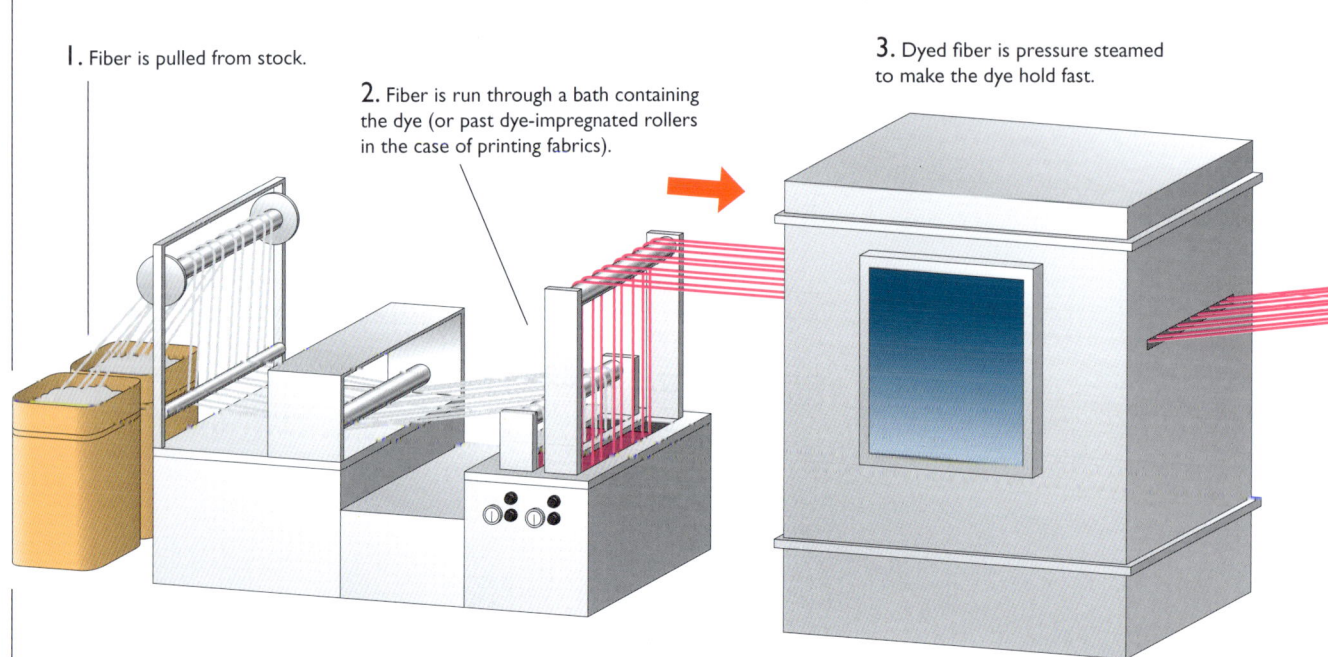

1. Fiber is pulled from stock.
2. Fiber is run through a bath containing the dye (or past dye-impregnated rollers in the case of printing fabrics).
3. Dyed fiber is pressure steamed to make the dye hold fast.

(Above) An example of a continuous disperse dyeing process.

This form of dyeing can also be done at lower temperatures by putting the dye into liquids such as benzene. A pad-dry heat technique allows the dye to be placed on the fabric without the need for a liquid carrier at all. It is the basis of printing fabrics.

Ingrain dyeing

To use aniline dyes on fabrics, two chemicals are formed separately. The dye-making chemical is put into a solution and then spread onto the textile. It is then dipped into a solution of the aniline. As soon as the aniline and the color-making chemical (called a coupler) react, the color of the dye comes through. It does not matter in which order the solutions are applied.

4. Dyed fiber is washed to remove surplus dye.

5. Fiber is wound onto spindles before being taken from the factory.

(Left and below) Printing on fabrics uses a dye-laden pad. It is called the pad-dry heat process.

(Above) Tiny spots of blue dye used to make whites look whiter.

Dyes used as fabric and paper brighteners

You can use a dye to create a color or to mask a color. In the laundry and paper industries chemicals are also used to make washed clothes or paper look brighter.

Natural fibers tend to have a yellowish tinge. That is because the fibers absorb some parts of the light and not others. It is the yellower part of the color range that natural fibers reflect.

One way to make the fibers look whiter—which is what people mainly prefer—is to use a bleach. However, bleach also reacts with the fibers and can harm them. If a light blue dye is added to the water and absorbed by clothes or paper, then it balances out the yellowish tinge and produces a whiter appearance. Many laundry powders contain a blue dye for just this purpose.

Alternatively, a slightly fluorescent dye can be added. It gives out a pale blue light, again balancing the natural yellow in the materials. All of these colorants are known as BRIGHTENERS.

(Below) Food coloring sold for cooking.

Dyes as food colorings

We like food not just because it tastes good, but because it feels good, smells good, and looks good. One of the most important factors is looking good, and part of the reason for this is that the food has an attractive color.

We are very sensitive to the color of food because it tells us whether a food is of high or poor quality, whether it is ripe, overripe, or bad, and whether it has been damaged in any way.

Colorants are used in food in part because food processing tends to take away the color that food has when it is fresh (the pigments undergo a chemical change that weakens their intensity of color), and in part to make it an attractive color so that we look forward to eating it. Colorants are also used to give the whole food an even color—an important factor when food is being produced on a conveyor belt.

Changing the color can be a matter of adding or removing color. For example, natural flour used for bread would produce a pale fawn-colored loaf. That is not what some customers want. To make bread white, the color needs to be removed. In this case the natural dye in the wheat is taken out by using a bleach. It OXIDIZES the food dye to a colorless form.

(Above) Coloring is widespread in the food industry using dyes that are harmless. They are used here to color icing decoration.

(*Above and below*) Food that has been colored: checkerboard cake and glacé cherries.

To make brown bread, manufacturers often start with white flour (that has been bleached) and add a dye to make it an attractive brown color. So a wholesome-looking brown loaf (not wholemeal) may have been processed with two chemicals just for the sake of appearances.

Other foods that commonly contain colorants are soft drinks, sweets, chocolates, ice cream, and processed snacks.

Two kinds of colorants are now commonly used: those derived from natural materials, and those that are produced from crude oil.

Many traditional food dyes used natural mineral colors. They were metal oxides. Metal oxides may be safe, or they may, in the long term, be hazardous. In any case, government agencies look very hard at any additives put in food, and dyes and pigments are no exception.

Most of the natural colorants used today are extracted from plant tissues. The problem with using these colorants is that in themselves, they may vary in intensity, while they may also have a taste and smell of their own. They may also react with the food they are coloring.

Synthetic dyes have many advantages for the manufacturer over natural colorings. Their brightness, stability, and color range can all be closely controlled. The synthetic colorants used are all soluble in water. They produce more intense and reliable colors than natural colorants and have no taste or odor of their own.

The difficulty with using food dyes is that any health problem that might be caused may not be recognizable for many years. Countries around the world also do not agree on which dyes are safe in foods and which are not. Some countries will not allow any food dyes, but most countries allow a few. The commonly used ones are: erythrosin, indigotine, Fast Green FCF and Brilliant Blue FCF, Allura Red, Sunset Yellow FCF, tartrazine, and Citrus Red 2.

4: Paints, varnishes, and other protective coatings

Dyes are designed to color a material; they generally have no protective role at all. By contrast, PAINTS and some other coating materials have a dual role of color and protection.

Paints

The name paint is given to any surface coating that both colors and protects a surface. A paint consists of a colored substance, the pigment, and a material that will allow it to stick to the surface, known as a vehicle or BINDER. The purpose of the vehicle or binder—which is, for example, a RESIN-based substance dissolved in a solvent—is to form a hard, transparent protective film that holds the pigment to the surface.

Early paints borrowed the same coloring used in food dyes, but they also used ground-up

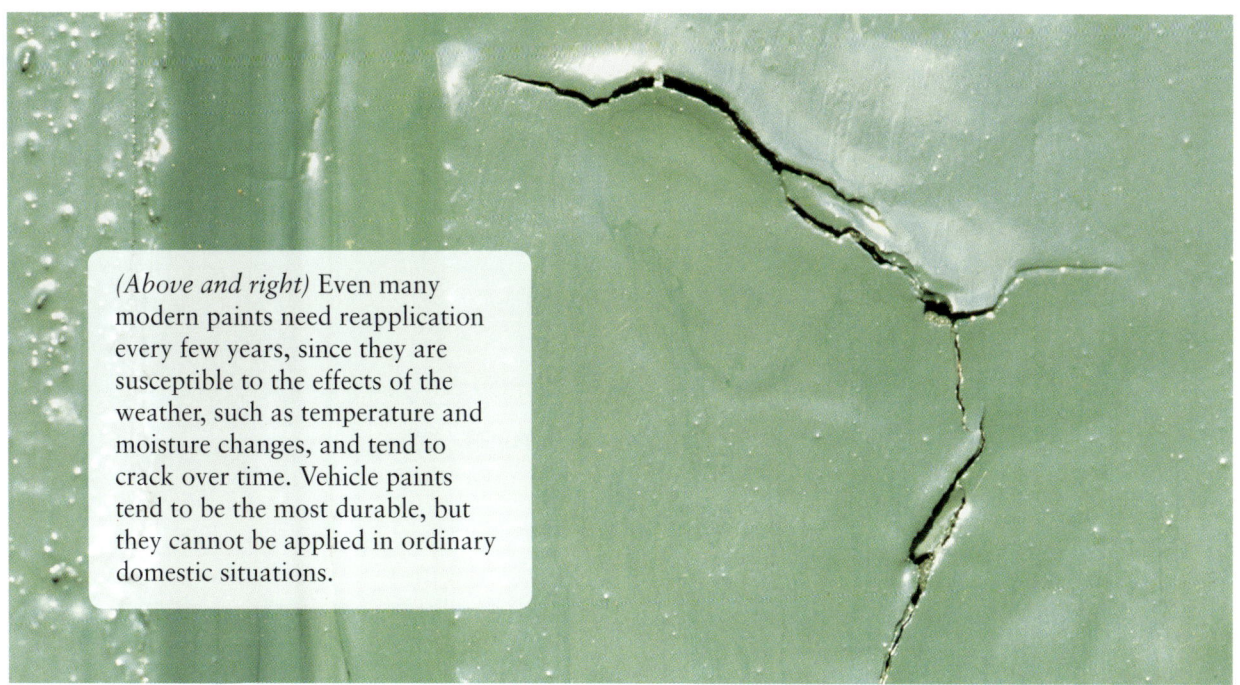

(Above and right) Even many modern paints need reapplication every few years, since they are susceptible to the effects of the weather, such as temperature and moisture changes, and tend to crack over time. Vehicle paints tend to be the most durable, but they cannot be applied in ordinary domestic situations.

See **Vol. 1: Plastics** and **Vol. 7: Fibers** for more on polymers.

colored rock. To hold the pigment to the surface, they used adhesive binders that varied from beeswax to egg white to gum arabic.

Paint making used exactly the same constituents for thousands of years. It was not until the 18th century that linseed oil was found to be a good binder (although very slow to evaporate). But the great revolution in paint making has come about since the early 20th century and has paralleled the developments in knowledge about polymers.

(Left and below) Older cars simply had a painted primer, an undercoat, and a top coat with lacquer. As a result, they were very prone to rust.

Modern cars have much better adhering pigments, and vulnerable areas (such as undersides and wheel wells) are further protected with a separate rubberized polymer layer. As a result, corrosion warranties have been able to be extended to 6 years and beyond. This dramatic increase in longevity of vehicle bodies has been entirely the result of improvements in surface coating techniques.

From the early 20th century a wide range of synthetic polymers was used as binders, coupled with a wide range of synthetic pigments.

The development of these new paints not only improved the ease of application of paint and its color, but also showed that paint could be used to help stop fires, prevent rusting, and so on.

Most of the paints produced in the early years of synthetic paints were based on resins. They are known as OIL-BASED PAINTS. It was not found possible to develop water-based paints that worked anything like as well. But more recently water-based paints have been developed based on LATEX, and they are now used for most "flat" (matt, silk, and eggshell) wall and ceiling paints and even for some shiny (gloss) finish paints.

The pigments in white paints are still dominated by zinc oxide, zinc sulfide, lithopone, and titanium dioxide. Most black paints use carbon. A wide variety of other colors are produced. Red pigments can be obtained by using iron oxides, yellow is a color produced by chromates, molybdates, and cadmium compounds, and so on.

(Above) Modern metallic coating protected with a melamine resin-based lacquer.

(Left) Flaking paint is a sign that the base paint coat has failed. The only proper solution is to strip off all the coats of paint and start again.

Preparation coats

In most cases multiple surface coatings are applied. That is because each coat has different properties. For example, when painting a fresh surface of wood on, for example, the siding of a house, the first coat is a primer. This coat of paint is absorbed into the wood grain. It must contain a high proportion of pigment because its main use is to block up the pores of the wood and mask the wood color. Most primers are white because white is a good base color for top coats.

An undercoat will be painted on top of the primer. The undercoat is more VISCOUS than the primer and is designed to provide a good base that the top coat can stick to. It is used to cover up any small irregularities in the surface of the wood that were not removed by initial sanding.

The final coat is the top coat. The top coat can be applied in one coat if the paint is very opaque and if applied in a sufficiently thick layer. But more usually, especially in exposed locations, two coats are put on because two thin coats produce a better finish. This coat has a high

(Above and below) A primer is a form of paint designed to seal the surface and form a bond between the undercoat and the surface being painted. It may also contain a fungicide and rust-preventing compounds if used on steel.

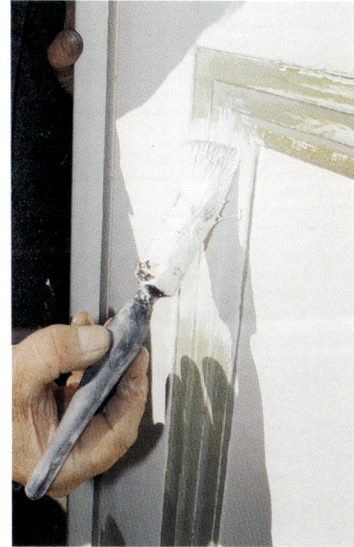

(*Above*) An undercoat is often an ALKYD-based paint similar to a gloss paint, which will form the topcoat. It is designed to help cover over other colors. It does not have a high gloss finish and is cheaper to manufacture. An undercoat followed by a top gloss coat is therefore cheaper than using two gloss coats.

(*Right and below*) Top coat— oil based or latex based. A high gloss finish is easy to clean and lets water run off.

binder content and is designed to withstand the weather. It provides the final color and type of finish.

In the end there are three layers of paint, each with a specific role in protecting the wood. Together they will provide a very durable finish.

(Above) Much exterior paint is acrylic stain with Teflon additives to help resist accumulation of grime.

Antirust paint

When painting iron and steel, the problem is to exclude moisture and air, because if this combination reaches the metal, then rust will quickly spread under the paint, lifting it from the surface. At the same time, the metal will be corroded away.

Red lead oxide or a phosphate are often the primers of choice in these circumstances. They react with the iron and

form chemical compounds that are inert and so do not react with air or water.

Once applied, they leave a dark-colored paint on the surface, and so an undercoat must then be applied before a final topcoat. The topcoat on metal is often made specially for the purpose; paint suitable for wood is often too viscous to be successfully applied to metal.

(Above) A red lead oxide primer is a form of paint designed to prevent rust forming on steel. The lead oxide coating completely seals in the steel. It also contains rust inhibitors such as phosphates. It is more effective than an ordinary wood primer and is used on outdoor metal surfaces.

(Right) Gloss paint for metal is an alkyd-based paint with a high gloss finish. The pigment is suspended in a solvent. A gloss paint dries much more slowly than an emulsion and gives off fumes as it dries. Gloss paint flows much more easily over nonporous surfaces than emulsion.

Modern paints and protective coatings

There is a wide variety of modern paints that can be used. Each type of paint can be produced with a variety of characteristics, particularly with a different luster finish, or SHEEN.

Flat paint has a nonshiny appearance. It is most often used on interior walls and ceilings.

Eggshell finish has a higher luster than flat, is usually an enamel paint, and is most often used on interior and exterior walls and on doors.

Satin has a bit more luster than eggshell. It is commonly used in kitchens, baths, and on interior doors because it is more washable than flat latex.

Semigloss is between very shiny and satin. It is commonly used in kitchens and on interior doors. It is very resistant to marking and easy to clean.

Gloss paint has a very shiny appearance and is commonly used on wood and metal where a high shine is needed. It is a common outdoor paint because it is easy to wipe clean.

Each of these characteristics can be produced from a variety of paints, as shown below.

(Above and below) Vinyl emulsion paint is water based and suitable for a top coat on interior walls and ceilings. It has little odor and contains no toxic materials. It dries to a water-resistant matte finish. It is not, however, suitable for less porous surfaces such as wood or metal.

Latex paint

LATEX PAINTS are modern water-based paints, also known as EMULSION PAINTS. On cans they might also sometimes be called latex stains or acrylic stains. They are environmentally less damaging than oil-based paints because they are soluble in water, so brushes are easily cleaned and do not release solvents that may pollute the atmosphere. They also dry faster than oil-based paints. They are used for walls and ceilings. Latex paints thin with water but are generally not thixotropic (that is, they are not nondrip but drip and spatter). They can be applied with synthetic brushes and rollers (but not natural bristles or lambswool rollers because they absorb the water and become

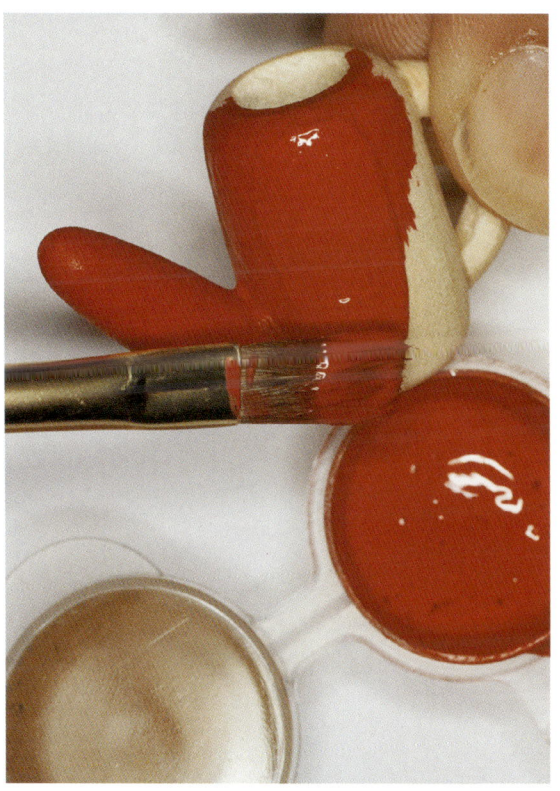

(Above, right, and below) Most craftwork paints are water-soluble acrylics.

soggy). Latex paint is cleaned with warm, soapy water. Latex paints do not have a highly reflective gloss finish.

Oil paint

Oil paint is the traditional paint used for wood and metal and is often called gloss paint. It is thinned with solvents such as mineral spirits or turpentine. Brushes and rollers also have to be cleaned with a suitable solvent; water and soap have little effect.

Oil-based paints dry more slowly than latex paints, and they have a strong odor while drying. They tend to produce a better gloss finish than latex paints. They can be used indoors or out.

(Above and below)
A variety of stains can be applied directly to wood when a painted surface is not required. The inset picture above shows tar-based creosote, the traditional wood preservative. The pictures above and below show the application of a modern water-based equivalent.

Preservatives

Paints are designed to stain and to protect using thick surface coatings that look attractive. But they are not always required. On shingle roofs or fence posts, for example, it is sufficient to add a preservative. Often a stain (dye) is added to the preservative, but no pigment is added.

The traditional preservative of this kind is creosote. Creosote is a substance that comes from crude oil. It leaves a strong odor and a greasy surface. Although widely used in the past, these disadvantages have meant that it is less widely applied today, although it is still cheaper than the water-based and odor-free replacements.

Varnishes

A varnish contains only a resin, and so its main function is as a protective coating. When a varnish dries, it is transparent. To aid the application of a varnish, varnish contains not only resin but drying oils and a solvent, which evaporate after the varnish has been applied. As the solvent evaporates, the resin combines with the drying oil to produce a hard, scratch-resistant polymer.

You can see what is involved by looking at the process of producing a natural varnish. First, a natural resin, such as the one that leaks from some plants, is boiled with linseed oil until the mixture thickens. It is then diluted with turpentine. This traditional varnish dries very slowly and in the meantime can pick up dust, flies, and other airborne materials that can spoil the finish. The natural varnish also yellows and cracks with age. That is why natural varnishes have been replaced by synthetics such as alkyd, polyurethane, phenolic, vinyl, and epoxy resins.

The advantage of a varnish is not just that it protects, but also that it reflects light and so makes a surface appear glossy and richer. Varnishes are particularly applied to wood, both indoors on floors and outdoors on benches and boats.

(Left and above) Varnish is a resin that dries to a hard, transparent film. Synthetic varnishes can reduce cracking and remain clear. Synthetic varnishes are also quick drying. Polyurethane varnish wears better.

Enamels

An ENAMEL, in paint terms, means a varnish that has pigments added. It is used to produce a durable, easy to clean surface, for example, on home appliances such as stoves and refrigerators.

The word "enamel" was originally used for a glasslike coating on a metal object. The object was dipped in glass powder and then heated so that the powder melted to fuse it, set on cooling, and produce a hard coating—old-fashioned enamel baths and bowls are classic examples. The glass composites used had a low melting point to prevent damage to the metal and often contained pigment particles to add color to the enamel. Without these pigments they were more like transparent glazes through which the metal could be seen.

Because enamels are hard, protective, and corrosion resistant, the name has been taken over to some extent by paint makers, who use an organic resin (the binder) to contain pigment particles. Paint systems intended to be thick, protective, and hard wearing are often referred to as enamels or enamel paints, in part to suggest some of the good properties of actual inorganic enamels.

These paints often need some heat to drive the solvent off and cure the resins, for example, radiator paint, so they are less easy to use but have superior properties to the more "ordinary" paint. They have the advantage of easier application than real enamels, not needing the very high temperatures required to apply a glass coating, but the disadvantage of being less resistant to scuffs and blows and less able to resist the weather.

(Left and right) Enamel paint is designed to be painted onto metal surfaces such as radiators and as a repair coat on white goods such as freezers where scratches or chips may have occurred.

(Above, right, and below) Reflective paints used for road markings and signs.

Reflective paints

There are many uses for a reflective paint in traffic control. Reflective paints are used on road signs and on road markings. Many are made with a durable binder that is applied hot and solidifies soon after application. It has to withstand continual wear by vehicles, and so the extra thickness applied is to ensure that repainting is not needed for some time.

Paints that are used in less extreme conditions may be sprayed on.

In both cases the reflective paint quality is produced by using minute glass beads. The beads work by total internal reflection of light. Whatever the angle of light that shines on a glass bead, it will enter the bead, be reflected twice inside, and come out again at the same angle as it entered. Thus when a car headlight shines on a glass bead, the bead reflects the light back toward the car.

Solid glass beads can be made simply by crushing glass in order to obtain a fine powder, or frit, then passing it through a hot flame. The angular powder fragments begin to melt and form balls. They are then cooled quickly to maintain their shape.

Powder coatings

A major breakthrough in the use of pigments has been in POWDER COATING. Vehicles, bicycles, and domestic appliances such as refrigerators are now all powder coated, not painted.

In powder coating an object is coated with a spray or placed in a bed of fluidized particles of polymer (plastic) pigment. To make sure an even coating is applied to all of the surface, electrical attraction is often used: The object being sprayed is given a charge opposite that of the powder. The particles are then fused to the surface by heating the object until the pigment particles melt and form a continuous film. In this process there is no solvent and no binder. Fusing also produces an extremely hard-wearing and weather-resistant coat. The powder coating is extremely thin. For durability in outdoor environments, therefore, the powder coating is protected by a melamine-based colorless lacquer. Powder coating the clear top coat using acrylic powders has now proved to be possible as well. This is a new process first developed in 1997.

(Above) Many bicycle frames are powder coated and lacquered; others are spray painted.

(Below) The powder-coating process using robots.

5: Adhesives

Adhesives are coatings that stick materials together by surface contact.

Just think of the things around you that are stuck together, and you will see why people have always looked for some kind of adhesive. The pages of this book are attached to their binding by adhesive; the fibers of the paper are held together by adhesive; many of the parts of a car are fastened together by adhesive; the wallcoverings in your house are held on by adhesive; the cartons that your groceries come in are held together with adhesives. The list is practically endless.

Adhesives are in common use because it takes much longer to fasten parts together with, for example, nuts and bolts than it does to stick them together. As a result, the pressure to mass produce things has made scientists try to find new types of adhesive, especially CONTACT ADHESIVES that will stick fast immediately when parts are put together.

When weight is critical, as it is in, for example, aircraft manufacture, there is again an incentive to develop reliable and very strong adhesives.

The term "adhesive," however, covers an enormous range of substances. They can be made from minerals, such as cement used to hold up buildings, or from GLUE (the adhesive extracted by boiling animal tissues such as bones and skins), or they can be made by modifying plastics.

The terms "adhesive" and "glue" are often used interchangeably in general conversation; but glue is now just one of an enormous variety of adhesives available, and in this book we will only use the word "glue" when taking about animal-based adhesives.

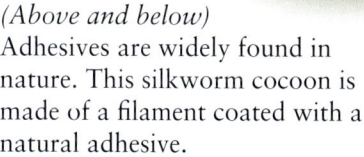

(Above and below)
Adhesives are widely found in nature. This silkworm cocoon is made of a filament coated with a natural adhesive.

A spider weaves a filament that is naturally sticky so that it can catch insects.

The history of adhesives

It is not hard to find nature's adhesives as you will have noticed if you accidentally walk into a spider's web. Many things we regularly use also have adhesive qualities. Dough sticks to the fingers when it is being made, and a flour-and-water paste sticks strips of newspaper to make papier-mâché models.

The whites of eggs are also naturally sticky substances and are often used as adhesives by cooks.

In monasteries monks used egg whites as an adhesive to stick down gold leaf onto hand-made illuminated books.

For centuries people made adhesives from fish, horns, bones, hides, and even milk and cheese.

People have found adhesives invaluable because it is not always desirable to tie things together with string or to use screws or bolts. In ancient Egypt glues were already in wide use to attach wood VENEERS to furniture.

Papyrus, the material the Egyptians used as an early form of paper, was made from reed fibers. These fibers when crushed exude a natural adhesive. They were also fastened together using a kind of flour-based PASTE.

(Above and below) Making papier-mâché.

See **Vol. 3: Wood and paper** for more on paper and wood veneers.

See **Vol. 1: Plastics** for more on polymers.

(Right) The surface of this papier-mâché box is protected from wear by using a lacquer and painting the surface.

The first synthetic adhesives were produced in the 19th century, when rubber- and nitrocellulose-based adhesives were introduced. Then, in the 20th century a far wider range of adhesives was produced because scientists realized that the polymers used for plastics could also be made into extremely versatile adhesives.

But from early times people did not just use adhesives to fasten things together. They also used them as the waterproof surface coatings we would now call SEALANTS. Bitumen, the pitch from some trees, and beeswax were both used as sealants (adhesive protective coatings).

Making adhesives work

Adhesives work either by creating strong chemical bonds between the adhesive and the materials it is sticking together or by solidifying in the pores of the material to be bonded. For those adhesives in which chemical bonding is important, this means that the chemical reactions must be given the chance to take place.

Three things are equally important in deciding on the strength and life of a joint that has been stuck together by an adhesive:
- the materials being stuck,
- the properties of the adhesive, and
- the size and shape of the surfaces being fastened.

Some adhesives are stronger than the materials they fasten. As a result, once stuck, the parts break apart within the material being joined, not through the adhesive.

(Below) Adhesive (loosely called "glue" by the manufacturer) used for a repair by sticking the upper to the sole of a shoe. It has to be at least as good as the stitching it replaces. This adhesive contains an isocyanate.

The sequence of pictures on these pages shows an adhesive that is stronger than the materials it is fastening. *(Right)* The adhesive is applied to the back of a wall tile, and the tile is attached to the wall. *(Below)* Once the tile adhesive has set, it takes a considerable force using a chisel to dislodge it. *(Far right)* Notice that the chiseling brings tile, adhesive, and part of the wall away. The break is not at the adhesive.

There are two separate mechanism involved in adhesion: physical and chemical. Physical processes are usually the most important, with chemical reaction playing a subsidiary role. People can be disappointed in the performance of an adhesive because they have not only replaced nuts and bolts with an adhesive, but they have changed the nature of the joint as well, very often putting far more stress on the joint than was there before.

How adhesives work

When molecules get very close together, they can attract one another very strongly. The adhesive is made of a material that is strongly attracted by the substances it is to join.

Once the molecules of the adhesive are touching, they attract one another by very powerful forces called valency forces. No chemical reaction is involved, that is, no electrons or ions are swapped. It is simply an attraction much as when a magnet is brought close to a piece of steel, but the attraction is often more powerful than the forces holding the materials together.

Surface attraction is probably the most important cause of ADHESION, but some other causes are important, too, although not all work in every case.

First, no surfaces are perfectly smooth; they have small bumps and troughs in them. Very often they have tiny holes that go deep into the material. If an adhesive can get into these holes and set hard, that helps hold the adhesive better.

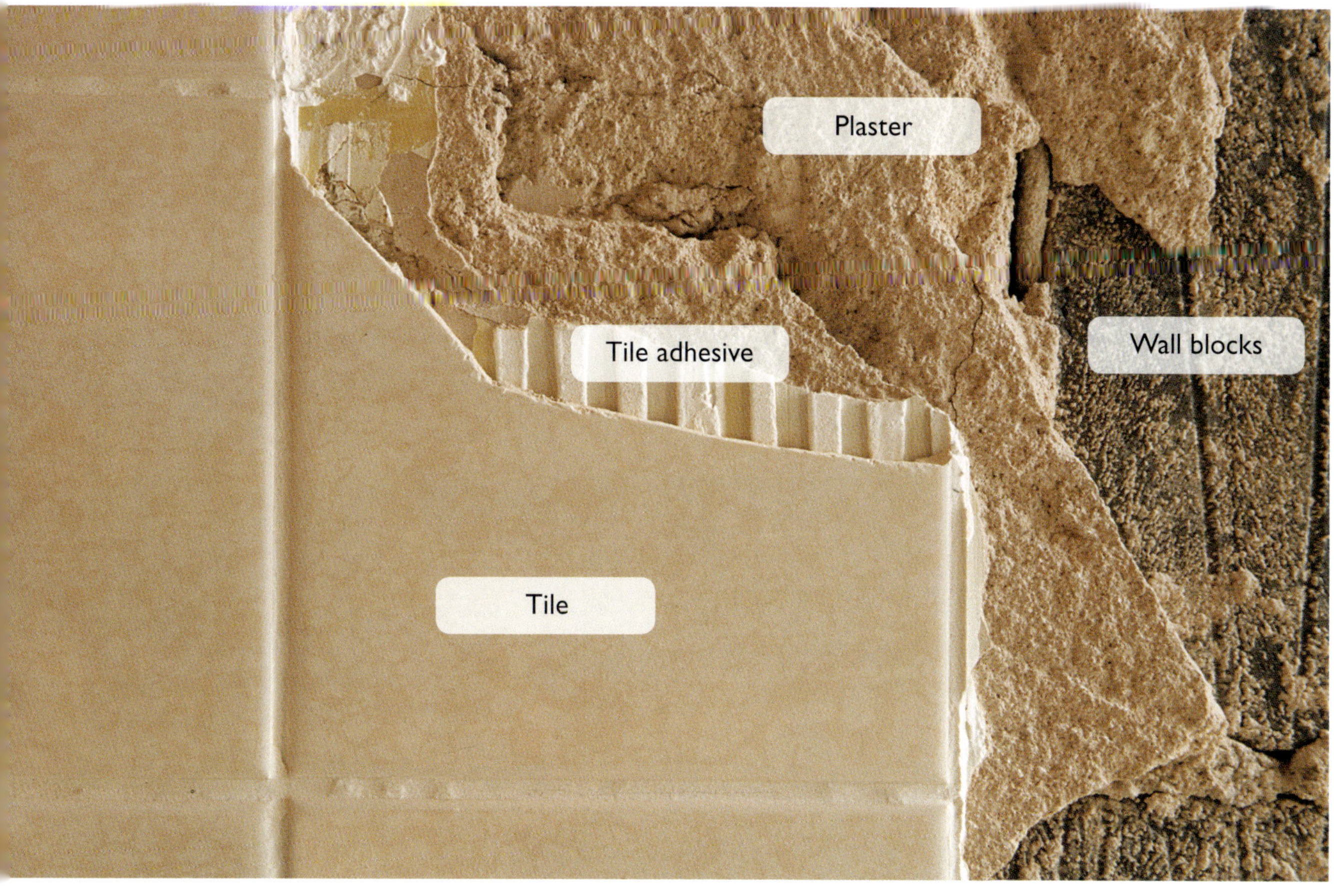

That is why roughened surfaces often stick better than smooth, polished ones.

Second, the adhesive sometimes also dissolves in the material when it is put onto it. In this way is becomes part of the material it is fastening.

Third, sometimes the molecules of the adhesive react chemically with the material they are spread on.

"Wetting" the surfaces

Whatever the cause of the adhesion, if an adhesive is to work well, it must easily spread out across the surfaces that are going to be joined. This is called WETTING, although in most cases no water is involved.

The reason for this is that the molecules of the adhesive must touch the molecules of the material being joined.

Even a single layer of molecules of grease, for example, will make it impossible

(Below) An adhesive works by attaching its molecules to molecules of the surfaces to be bonded.

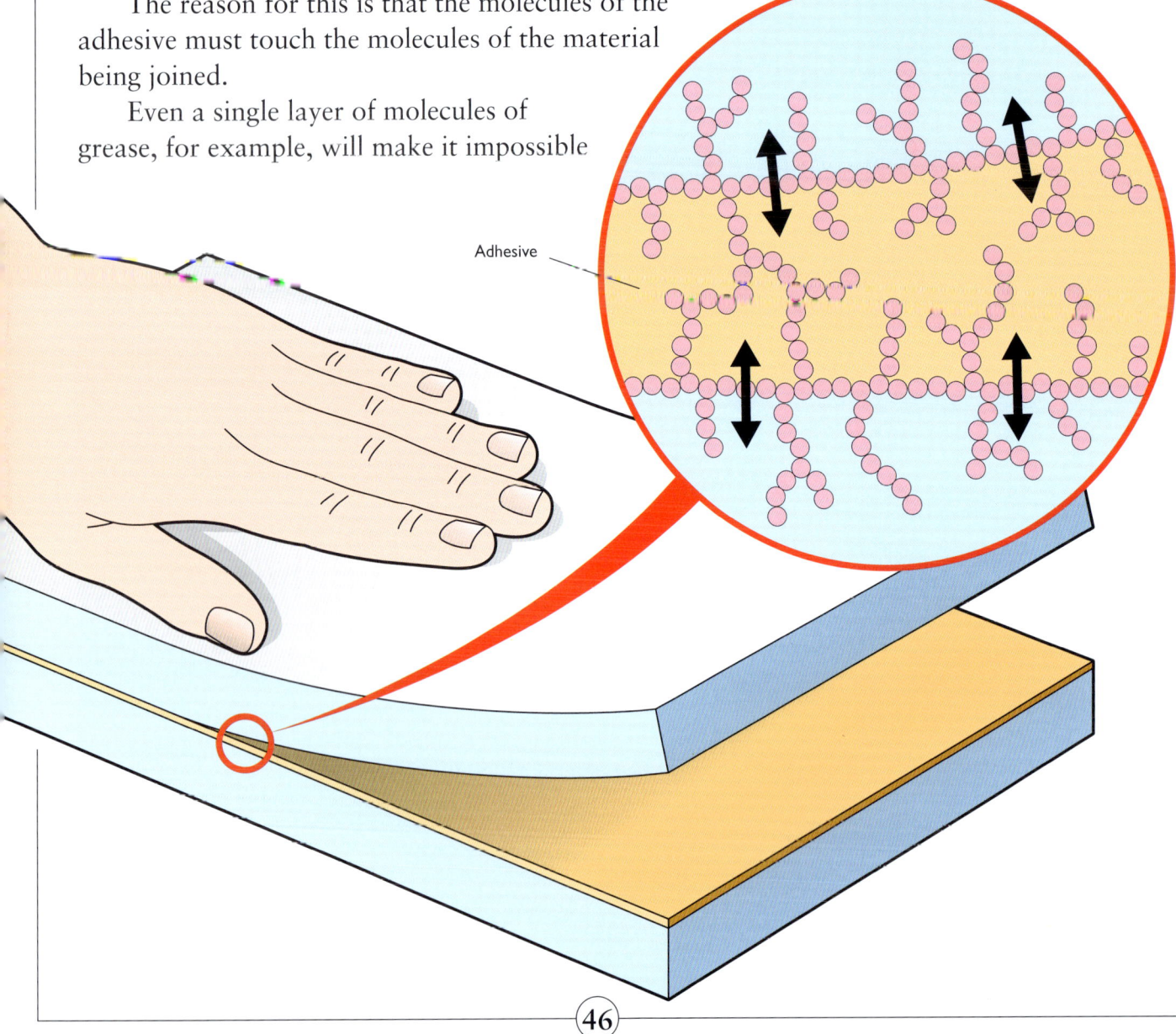

Adhesive

(Above) Wallpaper adhesive is often based on a corn extract, a natural adhesive. To make it stick, you add the adhesive to water and then paste it onto the paper. The paper is put on the wall and left to dry.

To get it off, you make the wallpaper wet again, and the adhesive dissolves.

However, this presents a problem for vinyl wallpapers because they do not let the wet in. Because the adhesive works so well, it is difficult to get VINYL wallpaper off when it is time to replace it. To get past this problem, the manufacturers make the wallpaper of two sheets pressed together. When the surface vinyl sheet is pulled, it comes away from the backing. The backing can then be made wet and the remaining wallpaper removed.

to get a good join. That is why adhesive instructions emphasize that the surfaces must be clean, grease-free, dry, and free from dust. If they are not, the adhesive will stick to the dust or be repelled by the grease or water.

Applying adhesives sparingly

Where the adhesive touches the material it is fastening, the surfaces make very tough joints. But many people think that by applying an extra thickness of adhesive, they will get a better, stronger joint. That is not true. In fact, the reverse is more likely to happen.

When the adhesive is thick, much of it is not close to the material it is sticking. The strength of the sticking then depends not on the adhesive properties but on how strong the adhesive itself is. In fact, this

(Above) An adhesive works by surface attractive forces and chemical reactions—a thin layer is often stronger than a thick layer, even though we may instinctively feel the opposite ought to be true.

is often the weakest part of the joint, and many joints fail within the adhesive, not at the joint—but only when too thick a layer of adhesive has been applied against the manufacturer's instructions. As a result, a thin layer of adhesive spread over a clean, grease-free surface will produce a better and stronger joint than a thick layer, as well as costing less in materials.

Natural adhesives

Adhesive materials can be formed from both plants and animals. These adhesives have been in use for thousands of years, and some are still employed widely today. Natural adhesives are also formed from materials that are renewable, and so they are environmentally more friendly. Most are called glues.

Glue from animal hides and bones

The most widely used is animal glue obtained from boiling bones and hides. The material collagen, which forms the basis of animal glue, is found in proteins of skin, bone, and muscle. Collagen is not soluble unless it is boiled or treated with alkalis or acids.

It is possible to make the collagen change only slightly. When this happens, the polymers remain large. We call this substance gelatin, and it is used as a glue in foods.

By boiling harder or using acids and alkalis, the collagen can be made to break down further. This produces the adhesive we called animal glue. The same kind of glue can also be obtained from fish bones.

Milk (casein) glue
Casein is a protein found in milk. It is extracted by using an alkali. It makes a stronger glue than animal glue and does not stain. It is used in paints, surface coatings, and where animal glue might previously have been used, such as in paper making and in bonding furniture.

Blood glue
One of the substances in the blood is a natural adhesive called albumen. It is obtained from animal blood and recovered from slaughterhouses. It is used in the plywood industry.

Potato and corn glue
Starch is one of the main substances in many kinds of corm and also root vegetables. It is a material that naturally flows from these foods during cooking and that colors the water white. This is especially noticeable when draining cooked rice.

This kind of adhesive will dissolve in water, and it is widely used in making wallpaper adhesive.

Gum
Certain plants will leak sap when their bark is cut. This is a natural adhesive known as gum. Gum arabic comes from tropical acacia trees. Rubber (latex), which leaks from rubber trees, can also be used as a natural adhesive. Gums are often used for the adhesive on stamps or the flaps of envelopes, which have to be licked before sealing.

Synthetic adhesives
Today, the majority of adhesives are synthetic, made by modifying the same materials that make plastics. They are called polymers, and each molecule consists of huge chains of linked atoms.

The key to adhesion lies in using polymers that will link with any materials they touch.

(Above) When you lick an envelope, you may be licking gum arabic. This water-based adhesive is very useful because it can be left in a dry, nonsticky state until needed. Then it is made wet simply by licking it.

See **Vol. 1: Plastics** for more on polymers.

There are six types of adhesive commonly used:
- epoxy resins, which are very strong, rigid, and stand up to high temperatures and liquids;
- polyurethane, which is a more flexible adhesive often used in foam form;
- acrylic, used where the materials to be stuck may be oily;
- anaerobics, which are adhesives that cure under water and in airless places such as threads of bolts;
- cyanoacrylates, which can fasten plastics and rubber;
- silicones, which are almost inert and are used as sticky sealants.

Like polymers, synthetic adhesives are either thermoplastic or thermosetting materials. Thermoplastic adhesives can be softened on warming. Acrylics are common thermoplastic adhesives. Thermosetting plastics, on the other hand, set once and for all. The epoxy resins are a common thermoset.

How common adhesives are used

Epoxy resins

These adhesive polymers can be formed by the reaction of two substances that are not themselves sticky. When they are mixed together, they form an adhesive polymer.

Epoxy resins are adhesives that develop their strength as they react, or "cure," after mixing.

(Above) A typical thermoplastic adhesive is used on the back of iron-on strips of wood laminate. Applying the iron to an already attached piece of laminate allows it to be repositioned.

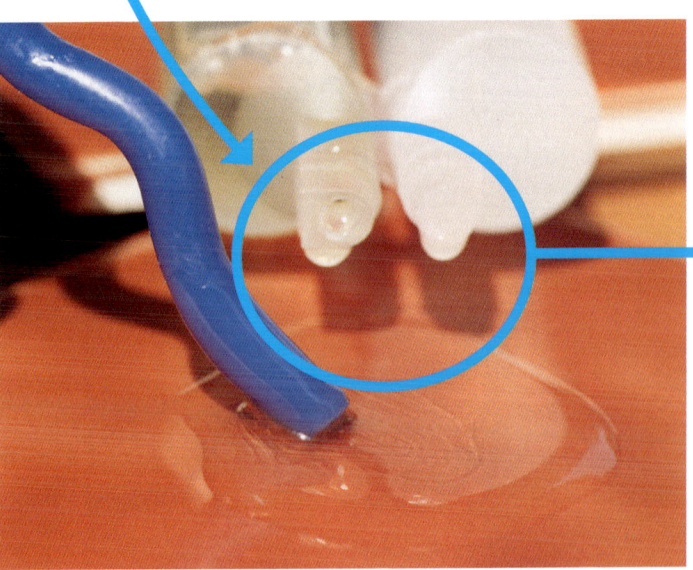

(Right) Many epoxy resins are two-part liquids.

(Above, left, and below) A two-part epoxy resin is used to make a filler for wood under the general name "plastic wood." Car repairers use the "plastic metal" formulation to fill in minor dents.

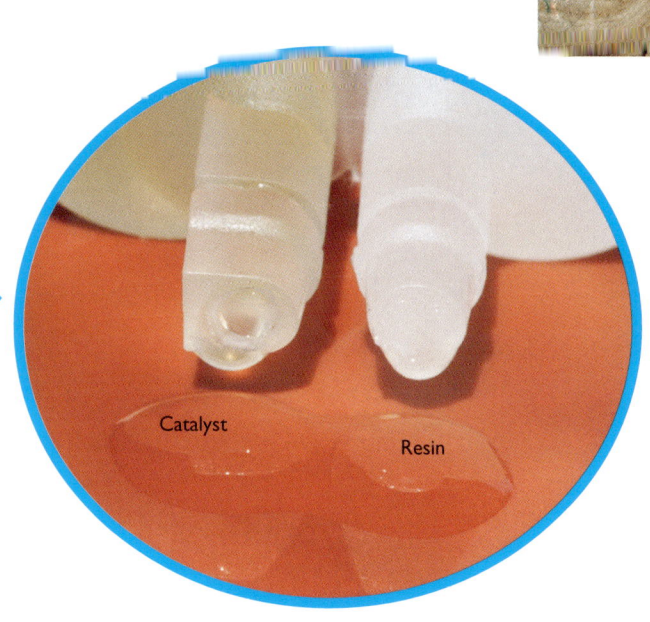

Catalyst   Resin

Contact adhesives

Contact adhesives are sticky from the moment they are made.

Many contact adhesives are made using rubber or neoprene in a solvent. They are spread over the surfaces that are to be bonded, and the solvent is allowed to evaporate. Once the surfaces are brought into contact, they form a very strong, flexible physical bond. They can be used in car manufacture (where adhesives need to stand up to the constant vibration and shaking due to movement) and in holding down carpets. They will stick leather to wood and plastics to plastics.

It is possible to buy contact adhesives in a spray gun. In this case the adhesive is dissolved in a solvent, and the solvent evaporates once the adhesive is sprayed onto a surface. Adhesives used to mount photos are an example. The adhesive is sprayed onto the two surfaces to be joined, and then the surfaces are brought together for an instant bond. This adhesive dries very quickly.

(Below) Photo contact spray for mounting pictures on paper.

(Above) Contact adhesives can be used to fasten carpet to flooring.

(Below) Contact adhesives can come on the back of a plastic tape.

Repositionables

Under this heading come repositionable adhesives such as found in Post-it® Notes. These are made from minute balls of contact adhesive. They stick lightly and can be repositioned because the tiny balls limit the amount of surface area in contact between the adhesive and the material it is being stuck on to.

Adhesive tapes (PSAs)

There is a wide range of uses for adhesive tapes and pads. They are known as pressure-sensitive adhesives. Depending on the application, a range of adhesives are used, including rubbers, polyacrylates, and silicones. The adhesive is applied to a film of plastic, metal foil, or paper. PSAs are used for gluing parcels or for dressing wounds, among other things.

Super glue

Super glue is a cyanoacrylate adhesive that bonds in seconds as its solvent evaporates. However, it requires room temperature or higher for curing and so is useless in cold situations. When fixing two broken pieces of china cup, for example, a small drop of adhesive is applied to one part of the crack. When both parts are pushed together, capillary action draws the adhesive into the join.

(*Above*) A super glue style adhesive being used to repair a ceramic cup handle. (*Below*) The joint is strong but on close inspection is not without blemish because the break produced rough surfaces.

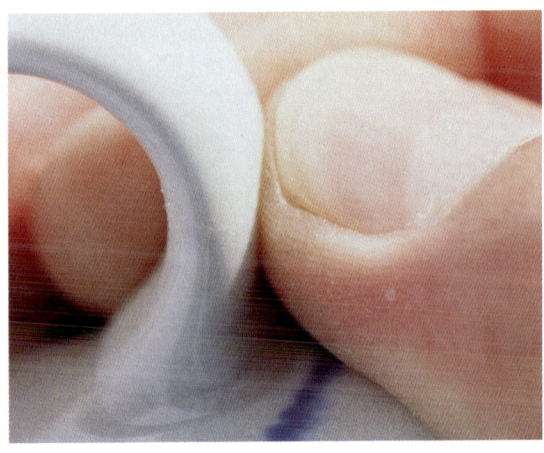

PVA adhesive

PVA is often called white glue. PVA stands for polyvinyl acetate. It is among the most common adhesives that can be bought in stores.

PVAs need to be sucked into the surfaces they are bonding by CAPILLARY ACTION. This means that they will only work with porous

(Above and below) PVA glue is often used for sticking dowels into holes in woodwork. It is often supplied with do-it-yourself furniture.

materials, so they are fine for bonding wood or fastening paper, but useless on plastics.

PVAs are water-based and so cure by loss of water. This also means that any surplus can be wiped off with a wet cloth. At the same time, PVAs are not waterproof, so can only be used on indoor applications.

Usually PVA requires the materials to be held tight while the adhesive sets (perhaps over some hours). So it is fine for gluing dowels into furniture but not useful for something you need to hold while it sets. Again, because PVA is water-based, it will not tolerate freezing. Once frozen, the adhesive is ruined.

Glass adhesives

Adhesives that stick to glass are among the most elusive. The bond has to form with a nonporous material and also be transparent. Sticking rear-view mirrors to windshields is an example of the need for a glass adhesive.

These adhesives cure using ultraviolet light from the Sun. Naturally, they work better in summer than winter when the sunshine is stronger, but they will also cure using an ultraviolet light gun.

Silicone-based adhesives

Silicone-based adhesives come under a variety of names such as "Goop." They are good for sticking leather to fabrics and rubber. Most of the sealants used on window frames and around baths, showers, and sinks are silicone adhesives. They are completely inert and waterproof. They will also stick to glass (although they do not make a strong bond). Most of these adhesives are applied with a caulking gun. They come in a variety of colors and can also be painted.

(Below and right) Silicone-based adhesives used as sealants.

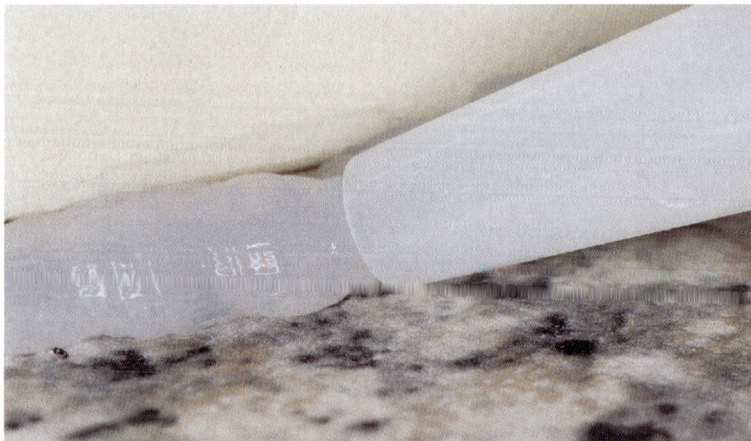

Silicone-based adhesives are used very widely in industry and often in large quantities; hence the sizes of the applicator guns are often larger (*below*) than those for domestic use (far *left*).

Adhesives for styrofoam (polystyrene)
Styrofoam (styrene, chlorodifluoroethane, and ethyl chloride) is widely used as a lightweight packaging material and insulator. It is remarkably easy to dissolve this material, and so no solvent-based adhesive can be used. It also melts at low temperatures and can give off toxic fumes, so a hot glue cannot be used. Water-based adhesives such as PVA are the only answer, but adhesive tape (especially double-sided tape) is often good enough because styrofoam has very low strength.

Set Glossary

ACID RAIN: Rain that falls after having been contaminated by acid gases produced by power plants, vehicle exhausts, and other man-made sources.

ACIDITY: The tendency of a liquid to behave like an acid, reacting with metals and alkalis.

ADDITION POLYMERIZATION: The building blocks of many plastics (or polymers) are simple molecules called monomers. Monomers can be converted into polymers by making the monomers link to one another to form long chains in head-to-tail fashion. This is called addition polymerization or chain polymerization. It is most often used to link vinyl monomers to produce, for example, PVC, or polyvinyl chloride polymer.
See also **CONDENSATION POLYMERIZATION**

ADHESIVE: Any substance that can hold materials together simply by using some kind of surface attachment. In some cases this is a chemical reaction; in other cases it is a physical attraction between molecules of the adhesive and molecules of the substance it sticks to.

ADOBE: Simple unbaked brick made with mud, straw, and dung. It is dried in the open air. In this form it is very vulnerable to the effects of rainfall and so is most often found in desert areas or alternatively is protected by some waterproof covering, for example, thatch, straw, or reeds.

ALKALI: A base, or substance that can neutralize acids. In glassmaking an alkali is usually potassium carbonate and used as a flux to lower the melting point of the silica.

ALKYD: Any kind of synthetic resin used for protective coatings such as paint.

ALLOY: A metal mixture made up of two or more elements. Most of the elements used to make an alloy are metals. For example, brass is an alloy of copper and zinc, but carbon is an exception and used to make steel from iron.

AMALGAM: An alloy of mercury and one or more other metals. Dentist's filling amalgam traditionally contains mercury, silver, and tin.

AMPHIBIOUS: Adapted to function on both water and land.

AMORPHOUS: Shapeless and having no crystalline form. Glass is an amorphous solid.

ANION: An ion with a negative charge.

ANNEALING: A way of making a metal, alloy, or glass less brittle and more easy to work (more ductile) by heating it to a certain temperature (depending on the metal), holding it at that temperature for a certain time, and then cooling to room temperature.

ANODIZING: A method of plating metal by electrically depositing an oxide film onto the surface of a metal. The main purpose is to reduce corrosion.

ANTICYCLONE: A region of the Earth's atmosphere where the pressure is greater than average.

AQUEOUS SOLUTION: A substance dissolved in water.

ARTIFACT: An object of a previous time that was created by humans.

ARTIFICIAL DYE: A dye made from a chemical reaction that does not occur in nature. Dyes made from petroleum products are artificial dyes.

ARTIFICIAL FIBER: A fiber made from a material that has been manufactured, and that does not occur naturally. Rayon is an example of an artificial fiber.
Compare to **SYNTHETIC**

ATMOSPHERE: The envelope of gases that surrounds the Earth.

ATOM: The smallest particle of an element; a nucleus and its surrounding electrons.

AZO: A chemical compound that contains two nitrogen atoms joined by a double bond and each linked to a carbon atom. Azo compounds make up more than half of all dyes.

BARK: The exterior protective sheath of the stem and root of a woody plant such as a tree or a shrub. Everything beyond the cambium layer.

BAROMETER: An instrument for measuring atmospheric pressure.

BASE METAL: Having a low value and poorer properties than some other metals. Used, for example, when describing coins that contain metals other than gold or silver.

BAST FIBERS: A strong woody fiber that comes from the phloem of plants and is used for rope and similar products. Flax is an example of a bast fiber.

BATCH: A mixture of raw materials or products that are processes in a tank or kiln. This process produces small amounts of material or products and can be contrasted to continuous processes. Batch processing is used to make metals, alloys, glass, plastics, bricks, and other ceramics, dyes, and adhesives.

BAUXITE: A hydrated impure oxide of aluminum. It is the main ore used to obtain aluminum metal. The reddish-brown color of bauxite is caused by impurities of iron oxides.

BINDER: A substance used to make sure the pigment in a paint sticks to the surface it is applied to.

BIOCERAMICS: Ceramic materials that are used for medical and dental purposes, mainly as implants and replacements.

BLAST FURNACE: A tall furnace charged with a mixture of iron ore, coke, and limestone and used for the refining (smelting) of iron ore. The name comes from the strong blast of air used during smelting.

BLOWING: Forming a glass object by blowing into a gob of molten glass to form a bubble on the end of a blowpipe.

BOLL: The part of the cotton seed that contains the cotton fiber.

BOILING POINT: The temperature at which a liquid changes to a vapor. Boiling points change with atmospheric pressure.

BOND: A transfer or a sharing of electrons by two or more atoms. There are a number of kinds of chemical bonds, some very strong, such as covalent bonding and ionic bonding, and others quite weak, as in hydrogen bonding. Chemical bonds form because the linked molecules are more stable than the unlinked atoms from which they are formed.

BOYLE'S LAW: At constant temperature and for a given mass of gas the volume of the gas is inversely proportional to the pressure that builds up.

BRITTLE: Something that has almost no plasticity and so shatters rather than bends when a force is applied.

BULL'S EYE: A piece of glass with concentric rings marking the place where the blowpipe was attached to the glass. It is the central part of a pane of crown glass.

BUOYANCY: The tendency of an object to float if it is less dense than the liquid it is placed in.

BURN: A combustion reaction in which a flame is produced. A flame occurs where gases combust and release heat and light. At least two gases are therefore required if there is to be a flame.

CALORIFIC: Relating to the production of heat.

CAMBIUM: A thin growing layer that separates the xylem and phloem in most plants, and that produces new cell layers.

CAPACITOR: An electronic device designed for the temporary storage of electricity.

CAPILLARY ACTION, CAPILLARITY: The process by which surface tension forces can draw a liquid up a fine-bore tube.

CARBOHYDRATES: One of the main constituents of green plants, containing compounds of carbon, hydrogen, and oxygen. The main kinds of carbohydrate are sugars, starches, and celluloses.

CARBON COMPOUNDS: Any compound that includes the element carbon. Carbon compounds are also called organic compounds because they form an essential part of all living organisms.

CARBON CYCLE: The continuous movement of carbon between living things, the soil, the atmosphere, oceans, and rocks, especially those containing coal and petroleum.

CAST: To pour a liquid metal, glass, or other material into a mold and allow it to cool so that it solidifies and takes on the shape of the mold.

CATALYST: A substance that speeds up a chemical reaction but itself remains unchanged. For example, platinum is used in a catalytic converter of gases in the exhausts leaving motor vehicles.

CATALYTIC EFFECT: The way a substance helps speed up a reaction even though that substance does not form part of the reaction.

CATHODIC PROTECTION: The technique of protecting a metal object by connecting it to a more easily oxidizable material. The metal object being protected is made into the cathode of a cell. For example, iron can be protected by coupling it with magnesium.

CATION: An ion with a positive charge, often a metal.

CELL: A vessel containing two electrodes and a liquid substance that conducts electricity (an electrolyte).

CELLULOSE: A form of carbohydrate. See **CARBOHYDRATE**

CEMENT: A mixture of alumina, silica, lime, iron oxide, and magnesium oxide that is burned together in a kiln and then made into a powder. It is used as the main ingredient of mortar and as the adhesive in concrete.

CERAMIC: A crystalline material. In a more everyday sense it is a material based on clay that has been heated so that it has chemically hardened.

CHARRING: To burn partly so that some of a material turns to carbon and turns black.

CHINA: A shortened version of the original "Chinese porcelain," it also refers to various porcelain objects such as plates and vases meant for domestic use.

CHINA CLAY: The mineral kaolinite, which is a very white clay used as the basis of porcelain manufacture.

CLAY MINERALS: The minerals, such as kaolinite, illite, and montmorillonite, that occur naturally in soils and some rocks, and that are all minute platelike crystals.

COKE: A form of coal that has been roasted in the absence of air to remove much of the liquid and gas content.

COLORANTS: Any substance that adds a color to a material. The pigments in paints and the chemicals that make dyes are colorants.

COLORFAST: A dye that will not "run" in water or change color when it is exposed to sunlight.

COMPOSITE MATERIALS: Materials such as plywood that are normally regarded as a single material, but that themselves are made up of a number of different materials bonded together.

COMPOUND: A chemical consisting of two or more elements chemically bonded together, for example, calcium carbonate.

COMPRESSED AIR: Air that has been squashed to reduce its volume.

COMPRESSION: To be squashed.

COMPRESSION MOLDING: The shaping of an object, such as a headlight lens, which is achieved by squashing it into a mold.

CONCRETE: A mixture of cement and a coarse material such as sand and small stones.

CONDENSATION: The process of changing a gas to a liquid.

CONDENSATION POLYMERIZATION: The production of a polymer formed by a chain of reactions in which a water molecule is eliminated as every link of the polymer is formed. Polyester is an example.

CONDUCTION: (i) The exchange of heat (heat conduction) by contact with another object, or (ii) allowing the flow of electrons (electrical conduction).

CONDUCTIVITY: The property of allowing the flow of heat or electricity.

CONDUCTOR: (i) Heat—a material that allows heat to flow in and out of it easily. (ii) Electricity—a material that allows electrons to flow through it easily.

CONTACT ADHESIVE: An adhesive, that, when placed on the surface to be joined sticks on contact as the surfaces are placed firmly together.

CONVECTION: The circulating movement of molecules in a liquid or gas as a result of heating it from below.

CORRODE/CORROSION: A reaction usually between a metal and an acid or alkali in which the metal decomposes. The word is used in the sense of the metal being eaten away and dangerously thinned.

CORROSIVE: Causing corrosion, that is, the oxidation of a metal. For example, sodium hydroxide is corrosive.

COVALENT BONDING: The most common type of strong chemical bond, which occurs when two atoms share electrons. For example, oxygen O_2.

CRANKSHAFT: A rodlike piece of a machine designed to change linear into rotational motion or vice versa.

CRIMP: To cause to become wavy.

CRUCIBLE: A ceramic-lined container for holding molten metal, glass, and so on.

CRUDE OIL: A chemical mixture of petroleum liquids. Crude oil forms the raw material for an oil refinery.

CRYSTAL: A substance that has grown freely so that it can develop external faces.

CRYSTALLINE: A solid in which the atoms, ions, or molecules are organized into an orderly pattern without distinct crystal faces.

CURING: The process of allowing a chemical change to occur simply by waiting a while. Curing is often a process of reaction with water or with air.

CYLINDER GLASS: An old method of making window glass by blowing a large bubble of glass, then swinging it until it forms a cylinder. The ends of the cylinder are then cut off with shears and the sides of the cylinder allowed to open out until they form a flat sheet.

DECIDUOUS: A plant that sheds its leaves seasonally.

DECOMPOSE: To rot. Decomposing plant matter releases nutrients back to the soil and in this way provides nourishment for a new generation of living things.

DENSITY: The mass per unit volume (for example, g/c^3).

DESICCATE: To dry up thoroughly.

DETERGENT: A cleaning agent that is able to turn oils and dirts into an emulsion and then hold them in suspension so they can be washed away.

DIE: A tool for giving metal a required shape either by striking the object with the die or by forcing the object over or through the die.

DIFFUSION: The slow mixing of one substance with another until the two substances are evenly mixed. Mixing occurs because of differences in concentration within the mixture. Diffusion works rapidly with gases, very slowly with liquids.

DILUTE: To add more of a solvent to a solution.

DISSOCIATE: To break up. When a compound dissociates, its molecules break up into separate ions.

DISSOLVED: To break down a substance in a solution without causing a reaction.

DISTILLATION: The process of separating mixtures by condensing the vapors through cooling. The simplest form of distillation uses a Liebig condenser arranged with just a slight slope down to the collecting vessel. When the liquid mixture is heated and vapors are produced, they enter the water cooled condenser and then flow down the tube, where they can be collected.

DISTILLED WATER: Water that has its dissolved solids removed by the process of distillation.

DOPING: Adding an impurity to the surface of a substance in order to change its properties.

DORMANT: A period of inactivity such as during winter, when plants stop growing.

DRAWING: The process in which a piece of metal is pulled over a former or through dies.

DRY-CLEANED: A method of cleaning fabrics with nonwater-based organic solvents such as carbon tetrachloride.

DUCTILE: Capable of being drawn out or hammered thin.

DYE: A colored substance that will stick to another substance so that both appear to be colored.

EARLY WOOD: The wood growth put on the spring of each year.

EARTHENWARE: Pottery that has not been fired to the point where some of the clay crystals begin to melt and fuse together and is thus slightly porous and coarser than stoneware or porcelain.

ELASTIC: The ability of an object to regain its original shape after it has been deformed.

ELASTIC CHANGE: To change shape elastically.

ELASTICITY: The property of a substance that causes it to return to its original shape after it has been deformed in some way.

ELASTIC LIMIT: The largest force that a material can stand before it changes shape permanently.

ELECTRODE: A conductor that forms one terminal of a cell.

ELECTROLYSIS: An electrical-chemical process that uses an electric current to cause the breakup of a compound and the movement of metal ions in a solution. It is commonly used in industry for purifying (refining) metals or for plating metal objects with a fine, even metal coat.

ELECTROLYTE: An ionic solution that conducts electricity.

ELECTROMAGNET: A temporary magnet that is produced when a current of electricity passes through a coil of wire.

ELECTRON: A tiny, negatively charged particle that is part of an atom. The flow of electrons through a solid material such as a wire produces an electric current.

ELEMENT: A substance that cannot be decomposed into simpler substances by chemical means, for example, silver and copper.

EMULSION: Tiny droplets of one substance dispersed in another.

EMULSION PAINT: A paint made of an emulsion that is water soluble (also called latex paint).

ENAMEL: A substance made of finely powdered glass colored with a metallic oxide and suspended in oil so that it can be applied with a brush. The enamel is then heated, the oil burns away, and the glass fuses. Also used colloquially to refer to certain kinds of resin-based paint that have extremely durable properties.

ENGINEERED WOOD PRODUCTS: Wood products such as plywood sheeting made from a combination of wood sheets, chips or sawdust, and resin.

EVAPORATION: The change of state of a liquid to a gas. Evaporation happens below the boiling point.

EXOTHERMIC REACTION: A chemical reaction that gives out heat.

EXTRUSION: To push a substance through an opening so as to change its shape.

FABRIC: A material made by weaving threads into a network, often just referred to as cloth.

FELTED: Wool that has been hammered in the presence of heat and moisture to change its texture and mat the fibers.

FERRITE: A magnetic substance made of ferric oxide combined with manganese, nickel, or zinc oxide.

FIBER: A long thread.

FILAMENT: (i) The coiled wire used inside a light bulb. It consists of a high-resistance metal such as tungsten that also has a high melting point. (ii) A continuous thread produced during the manufacture of fibers.

FILLER: A material introduced in order to give bulk to a substance. Fillers are used in making paper and also in the manufacture of paints and some adhesives.

FILTRATE: The liquid that has passed through a filter.

FLOOD: When rivers spill over their banks and cover the surrounding land with water.

FLUID: Able to flow either as a liquid or a gas.

FLUORESCENT: A substance that gives out visible light when struck by invisible waves, such as ultraviolet rays.

FLUX: A substance that lowers the melting temperature of another substance. Fluxes are use in glassmaking and in melting alloys. A flux is used, for example, with a solder.

FORMER: An object used to control the shape or size of a product being made, for example, glass.

FOAM: A material that is sufficiently gelatinous to be able to contain bubbles of gas. The gas bulks up the substances, making it behave as though it were semirigid.

FORGE: To hammer a piece of heated metal until it changes to the desired shape.

FRACTION: A group of similar components of a mixture. In the petroleum industry the light fractions of crude oil are those with the smallest molecules, while the medium and heavy fractions have larger molecules.

FRACTIONAL DISTILLATION: The separation of the components of a liquid mixture by heating them to their boiling points.

FREEZING POINT: The temperature at which a substance undergoes a phase change from a liquid to a solid. It is the same temperature as the melting point.

FRIT: Partly fused materials of which glass is made.

FROTH SEPARATION: A process in which air bubbles are blown through a suspension, causing a froth of bubbles to collect on the surface. The materials that are attracted to the bubbles can then be removed with the froth.

FURNACE: An enclosed fire designed to produce a very high degree of heat for melting glass or metal or for reheating objects so they can be further processed.

FUSING: The process of melting particles of a material so they form a continuous sheet or solid object. Enamel is bonded to the surface of glass this way. Powder-formed metal is also fused into a solid piece. Powder paints are fused to the surface by heating.

GALVANIZING: The application of a surface coating of zinc to iron or steel.

GAS: A form of matter in which the molecules take no definite shape and are free to move around to uniformly fill any vessel they are put in. A gas can easily be compressed into a much smaller volume.

GIANT MOLECULES: Molecules that have been formed by polymerization.

GLASS: A homogeneous, often transparent material with a random noncrystalline molecular structure. It is achieved by cooling a molten substance very rapidly so that it cannot crystallize.

GLASS CERAMIC: A ceramic that is not entirely crystalline.

GLASSY STATE: A solid in which the molecules are arranged randomly rather than being formed into crystals.

GLOBAL WARMING: The progressive increase in the average temperature of the Earth's atmosphere, most probably in large part due to burning fossil fuels.

GLUE: An adhesive made from boiled animal bones.

GOB: A piece of near-molten glass used by glass-blowers and in machines to make hollow glass vessels.

GRAIN: (i) The distinctive pattern of fibers in wood. (ii) Small particles of a solid, including a single crystal.

GRAPHITE: A form of the element carbon with a sheetlike structure.

GRAVITY: The attractive force produced because of the mass of an object.

GREENHOUSE EFFECT: An increase in the global air temperature as a result of heat released from burning fossil fuels being absorbed by carbon dioxide in the atmosphere.

GREENHOUSE GAS: Any of various gases that contribute to the greenhouse effect, such as carbon dioxide.

GROUNDWATER: Water that flows naturally through rocks as part of the water cycle.

GUM: Any natural adhesive of plant origin that consists of colloidal polysaccharide substances that are gelatinous when moist but harden on drying.

HARDWOOD: The wood from a nonconiferous tree.

HEARTWOOD: The old, hard, nonliving central wood of trees.

HEAT: The energy that is transferred when a substance is at a different temperature than that of its surroundings.

HEAT CAPACITY: The ratio of the heat supplied to a substance compared with the rise in temperature that is produced.

HOLOGRAM: A three-dimensional image reproduced from a split laser beam.

HYDRATION: The process of absorption of water by a substance. In some cases hydration makes a substance change color, but in all cases there is a change in volume.

HYDROCARBON: A compound in which only hydrogen and carbon atoms are present. Most fuels are hydrocarbons, for example, methane.

HYDROFLUORIC ACID: An extremely corrosive acid that attacks silicate minerals such as glass. It is used to etch decoration onto glass and also to produce some forms of polished surface.

HYDROGEN BOND: A type of attractive force that holds one molecule to another. It is one of the weaker forms of intermolecular attractive force.

HYDROLYSIS: A reversible process of decomposition of a substance in water.

HYDROPHILIC: Attracted to water.

HYDROPHOBIC: Repelled by water.

IMMISCIBLE: Will not mix with another substance, for example, oil and water.

IMPURITIES: Any substances that are found in small quantities, and that are not meant to be in the solution or mixture.

INCANDESCENT: Glowing with heat, for example, a tungsten filament in a light bulb.

INDUSTRIAL REVOLUTION: The time, which began in the 18th century and continued through into the 19th century, when materials began to be made with the use of power machines and mass production.

INERT: A material that does not react chemically.

INORGANIC: A substance that does not contain the element carbon (and usually hydrogen), for example, sodium chloride.

INSOLUBLE: A substance that will not dissolve, for example, gold in water.

INSULATOR: A material that does not conduct electricity.

ION: An atom or group of atoms that has gained or lost one or more electrons and so developed an electrical charge.

IONIC BONDING: The form of bonding that occurs between two ions when the ions have opposite charges, for example, sodium ions bond with chloride ions to make sodium chloride. Ionic bonds are strong except in the presence of a solvent.

IONIZE: To change into ions.

ISOTOPE: An atom that has the same number of protons in its nucleus, but that has a different mass, for example, carbon 12 and carbon 14.

KAOLINITE: A form of clay mineral found concentrated as china clay. It is the result of the decomposition of the mineral feldspar.

KILN: An oven used to heat materials. Kilns at quite low temperatures are used to dry wood and at higher temperatures to bake bricks and to fuse enamel onto the surfaces of other substances. They are a form of furnace.

KINETIC ENERGY: The energy due to movement. When a ball is thrown, it has kinetic energy.

KNOT: The changed pattern in rings in wood due to the former presence of a branch.

LAMINATE: An engineered wood product consisting of several wood layers bonded by a resin. Also applies to strips of paper stuck together with resins to make such things as "formica" worktops.

LATE WOOD: Wood produced during the summer part of the growing season.

LATENT HEAT: The amount of heat that is absorbed or released during the process of changing state between gas, liquid, or solid. For example, heat is absorbed when liquid changes to gas. Heat is given out again as the gas condenses back to a liquid.

LATEX: A general term for a colloidal suspension of rubber-type material in water. Originally for the milky white liquid emulsion found in the Para rubber tree, but also now any manufactured water emulsion containing synthetic rubber or plastic.

LATEX PAINT: A water emulsion of a synthetic rubber or plastic used as paint.
See **EMULSION PAINT**

LATHE: A tool consisting of a rotating spindle and cutters that is designed to produce shaped objects that are symmetrical about the axis of rotation.

LATTICE: A regular geometric arrangement of objects in space.

LEHR: The oven used for annealing glassware. It is usually a very long tunnel through which glass passes on a conveyor belt.

LIGHTFAST: A colorant that does not fade when exposed to sunlight.

LIGNIN: A form of hard cellulose that forms the walls of cells.

LIQUID: A form of matter that has a fixed volume but no fixed shape.

LUMBER: Timber that has been dressed for use in building or carpentry and consists of planed planks.

MALLEABLE: Capable of being hammered or rolled into a new shape without fracturing due to brittleness.

MANOMETER: A device for measuring liquid or gas pressure.

MASS: The amount of matter in an object. In common use the word weight is used instead (incorrectly) to mean mass.

MATERIAL: Anything made of matter.

MATTED: Another word for felted.
See **FELTED**

MATTER: Anything that has mass and takes up space.

MELT: The liquid glass produced when a batch of raw materials melts. Also used to describe molten metal.

MELTING POINT: The temperature at which a substance changes state from a solid phase to a liquid phase. It is the same as the freezing point.

METAL: A class of elements that is a good conductor of electricity and heat, has a metallic luster, is malleable and ductile, and is formed as cations held together by a sea of electrons. A metal may also be an alloy of these elements and carbon.

METAL FATIGUE: The gradual weakening of a metal by constant bending until a crack develops.

MINERAL: A solid substance made of just one element or compound, for example, calcite minerals contain only calcium carbonate.

MISCIBLE: Capable of being mixed.

MIXTURE: A material that can be separated into two or more substances using physical means, for example, air.

MOLD: A containing shape made of wood, metal, or sand into which molten glass or metal is poured. In metalworking it produces a casting. In glassmaking the glass is often blown rather than poured when making, for example, light bulbs.

MOLECULE: A group of two or more atoms held together by chemical bonds.

MONOMER: A small molecule and building block for larger chain molecules or polymers (mono means "one" and mer means "part").

MORDANT: A chemical that is attracted to a dye and also to the surface that is to be dyed.

MOSAIC: A decorated surface made from a large number of small colored pieces of glass, natural stone, or ceramic that are cemented together.

NATIVE METAL: A pure form of a metal not combined as a compound. Native metals are more common in nonreactive elements such as gold than reactive ones such as calcium.

NATURAL DYES: Dyes made from plants without any chemical alteration, for example, indigo.

NATURAL FIBERS: Fibers obtained from plants or animals, for example, flax and wool.

NEUTRON: A particle inside the nucleus of an atom that is neutral and has no charge.

NOBLE GASES: The members of group 8 of the periodic table of the elements: helium, neon, argon, krypton, xenon, radon. These gases are almost entirely unreactive.

NONMETAL: A brittle substance that does not conduct electricity, for example, sulfur or nitrogen.

OIL-BASED PAINTS: Paints that are not based on water as a vehicle. Traditional artists' oil paint uses linseed oil as a vehicle.

OPAQUE: A substance through which light cannot pass.

ORE: A rock containing enough of a useful substance to make mining it worthwhile, for example, bauxite, the ore of aluminum.

ORGANIC: A substance that contains carbon and usually hydrogen. The carbonates are usually excluded.

OXIDE: A compound that includes oxygen and one other element, for example, Cu_2O, copper oxide.

OXIDIZE, OXIDIZING AGENT: A reaction that occurs when a substance combines with oxygen or a reaction in which an atom, ion, or molecule loses electrons to another substance (and in this more general case does not have to take up oxygen).

OZONE: A form of oxygen whose molecules contain three atoms of oxygen. Ozone high in the atmosphere blocks harmful ultraviolet rays from the Sun, but at ground level it is an irritant gas when breathed in and so is regarded as a form of pollution. The ozone layer is the uppermost part of the stratosphere.

PAINT: A coating that has both decorative and protective properties, and that consists of a pigment suspended in a vehicle, or binder, made of a resin dissolved in a solvent. It dries to give a tough film.

PARTIAL PRESSURE: The pressure a gas in a mixture would exert if it alone occupied the flask. For example, oxygen makes up about a fifth of the atmosphere. Its partial pressure is therefore about a fifth of normal atmospheric pressure.

PASTE: A thick suspension of a solid in a liquid.

PATINA: A surface coating that develops on metals and protects them from further corrosion, for example, the green coating of copper carbonate that forms on copper statues.

PERIODIC TABLE: A chart organizing elements by atomic number and chemical properties into groups and periods.

PERMANENT HARDNESS: Hardness in the water that cannot be removed by boiling.

PETROCHEMICAL: Any of a large group of manufactured chemicals (not fuels) that come from petroleum and natural gas. It is usually taken to include similar products that can be made from coal and plants.

PETROLEUM: A natural mixture of a range of gases, liquids, and solids derived from the decomposed remains of animals and plants.

PHASE: A particular state of matter. A substance can exist as a solid, liquid, or gas and may change between these phases with the addition or removal of energy, usually in the form of heat.

PHOSPHOR: A material that glows when energized by ultraviolet or electron beams, such as in fluorescent tubes and cathode ray tubes.

PHOTOCHEMICAL SMOG: A mixture of tiny particles of dust and soot combined with a brown haze caused by the reaction of colorless nitric oxide from vehicle exhausts and oxygen of the air to form brown nitrogen dioxide.

PHOTOCHROMIC GLASSES: Glasses designed to change color with the intensity of light. They use the property that certain substances, for example, silver halide, can change color (and change chemically) in light. For example, when silver chromide is dispersed in the glass melt, sunlight decomposes the silver halide to release silver (and so darken the lens). But the halogen cannot escape; and when the light is removed, the halogen recombines with the silver to turn back to colorless silver halide.

PHOTOSYNTHESIS: The natural process that happens in green plants whereby the energy from light is used to help turn gases, water, and minerals into tissue and energy.

PIEZOELECTRICS: Materials that produce electric currents when they are deformed, or vice versa.

PIGMENT: Insoluble particles of coloring material.

PITH: The central strand of spongy tissue found in the stems of most plants.

PLASTIC: Material—a carbon-based substance consisting of long chains or networks (polymers) of simple molecules. The word plastic is commonly used only for synthetic polymers. Property—a material is plastic if it can be made to change shape easily and then remain in this new shape (contrast with elasticity and brittleness).

PLASTIC CHANGE: A permanent change in shape that happens without breaking.

PLASTICIZER: A chemical added to rubbers and resins to make it easier for them to be deformed and molded. Plasticizers are also added to cement to make it more easily worked when used as a mortar.

PLATE GLASS: Rolled, ground, and polished sheet glass.

PLIABLE: Supple enough to be repeatedly bent without fracturing.

PLYWOOD: An engineered wood laminate consisting of sheets of wood bonded with resin. Each sheet of wood has the grain at right angles to the one above and below. This imparts stability to the product.

PNEUMATIC DEVICE: Any device that works with air pressure.

POLAR: Something that has a partial electric charge.

POLYAMIDES: A compound that contains more than one amide group, for example, nylon.

POLYMER: A compound that is made of long chains or branching networks by combining molecules called monomers as repeating units. Poly means "many," mer means "part."

PORCELAIN: A hard, fine-grained, and translucent white ceramic that is made of china clay and is fired to a high temperature. Varieties include china.

PORES: Spaces between particles that are small enough to hold water by capillary action, but large enough to allow water to enter.

POROUS: A material that has small cavities in it, known as pores. These pores may or may not be joined. As a result, porous materials may or may not allow a liquid or gas to pass through them. Popularly, porous is used to mean permeable, the kind of porosity in which the pores are joined, and liquids or gases can flow.

POROUS CERAMICS: Ceramics that have not been fired at temperatures high enough to cause the clays to fuse and so prevent the slow movement of water.

POTENTIAL ENERGY: Energy due to the position of an object. Water in a reservoir has potential energy because it is stored up, and when released, it moves down to a lower level.

POWDER COATING: The application of a pigment in powder form without the use of a solvent.

POWDER FORMING: A process of using a powder to fill a mold and then heating the powder to make it fuse into a solid.

PRECIPITATE: A solid substance formed as a result of a chemical reaction between two liquids or gases.

PRESSURE: The force per unit area measured in SI units in Pascals and also more generally in atmospheres.

PRIMARY COLORS: A set of colors from which all others can be made. In transmitted light they are red, blue, and green.

PROTEIN: Substances in plants and animals that include nitrogen.

PROTON: A positively charged particle in the nucleus of an atom that balances out the charge of the surrounding electrons.

QUENCH: To put into water in order to cool rapidly.

RADIATION: The transmission of energy from one body to another without any contribution from the intervening space. Contrast with **CONVECTION** and **CONDUCTION**

RADIOACTIVE: A substance that spontaneously emits energetic particles.

RARE EARTHS: Any of a group of metal oxides that are found widely throughout the Earth's rocks, but in low concentrations. They are mainly made up of the elements of the lanthanide series of the periodic table of the elements.

RAW MATERIAL: A substance that has not been prepared, but that has an intended use in manufacturing.

RAY: Narrow beam of light

RAYON: An artificial fiber made from natural cellulose.

REACTION (CHEMICAL): The recombination of two substances using parts of each substance.

REACTIVE: A substance that easily reacts with many other substances.

RECYCLE: To take once used materials and make them available for reuse.

REDUCTION, REDUCING AGENT: The removal of oxygen from or the addition of hydrogen to a compound.

REFINING: Separating a mixture into the simpler substances of which it is made, especially petrochemical refining.

REFRACTION: The bending of a ray of light as it passes between substances of different refractive index (light-bending properties).

REFRACTORY: Relating to the use of a ceramic material, especially a brick, in high-temperature conditions of, for example, a furnace.

REFRIGERANT: A substance that, on changing between a liquid and a gas, can absorb large amounts of (latent) heat from its surroundings.

REGENERATED FIBERS: Fibers that have been dissolved in a solution and then recovered from the solution in a different form.

REINFORCED FIBER: A fiber that is mixed with a resin, for example, glass-reinforced fiber.

RESIN: A semisolid natural material that is made of plant secretions and often yellow-brown in color. Also synthetic materials with the same type of properties. Synthetic resins have taken over almost completely from natural resins and are available as thermoplastic resins and thermosetting resins.

RESPIRATION: The process of taking in oxygen and releasing carbon dioxide in animals and the reverse in plants.

RIVET: A small rod of metal that is inserted into two holes in metal sheets and then burred over at both ends in order to stick the sheets together.

ROCK: A naturally hard inorganic material composed of mineral particles or crystals.

ROLLING: The process in which metal is rolled into plates and bars.

ROSIN: A brittle form of resin used in varnishes.

RUST: The product of the corrosion of iron and steel in the presence of air and water.

SALT: Generally thought of as sodium chloride, common salt; however, more generally a salt is a compound involving a metal. There are therefore many "salts" in water in addition to sodium chloride.

SAPWOOD: The outer, living layers of the tree, which includes cells for the transportation of water and minerals between roots and leaves.

SATURATED: A state in which a liquid can hold no more of a substance dissolved in it.

SEALANTS: A material designed to stop water or other liquids from penetrating into a surface or between surfaces. Most sealants are adhesives.

SEMICONDUCTOR: A crystalline solid that has an electrical conductivity part way between a conductor and an insulator. This material can be altered by doping to control an electric current. Semiconductors are the basis of transistors, integrated circuits, and other modern electronic solid-state devices.

SEMIPERMEABLE MEMBRANE: A thin material that acts as a fine sieve or filter, allowing small molecules to pass, but holding back large molecules.

SEPARATING COLUMN: A tall glass tube containing a porous disk near the base and filled with a substance such as aluminum oxide that can absorb materials on its surface. When a mixture passes through the columns, fractions are retarded by differing amounts so that each fraction is washed through the column in sequence.

SEPARATING FUNNEL: A pear-shaped glass funnel designed to permit the separation of immiscible liquids by simply pouring off the more dense liquid from the bottom of the funnel, while leaving the less dense liquid in the funnel.

SHAKES: A defect in wood produced by the wood tissue separating, usually parallel to the rings.

SHEEN: A lustrous, shiny surface on a yarn. It is produced by the finishing process or may be a natural part of the yarn.

SHEET-METAL FORMING: The process of rolling out metal into sheet.

SILICA: Silicon dioxide, most commonly in the form of sand.

SILICA GLASS: Glass made exclusively of silica.

SINTER: The process of heating that makes grains of a ceramic or metal a solid mass before it becomes molten.

SIZE: A glue, varnish, resin, or similar very dilute adhesive sealant used to block up the pores in porous surfaces or, for example, plaster and paper. Once the size has dried, paint or other surface coatings can be applied without the coating sinking in.

SLAG: A mixture of substances that are waste products of a furnace. Most slag are mainly composed of silicates.

SMELTING: Roasting a substance in order to extract the metal contained in it.

SODA: A flux for glassmaking consisting of sodium carbonate.

SOFTWOOD: Wood obtained from a coniferous tree.

SOLID: A rigid form of matter that maintains its shape regardless of whether or not it is in a container.

SOLIDIFICATION: Changing from a liquid to a solid.

SOLUBILITY: The maximum amount of a substance that can be contained in a solvent.

SOLUBLE: Readily dissolvable in a solvent.

SOLUTION: A mixture of a liquid (the solvent) and at least one other substance of lesser abundance (the solute). Like all mixtures, solutions can be separated by physical means.

SOLVAY PROCESS: Modern method of manufacturing the industrial alkali sodium carbonate (soda ash).

SOLVENT: The main substance in a solution.

SPECTRUM: A progressive series arranged in order, for example, the range of colors that make up visible light as seen in a rainbow.

SPINNERET: A small metal nozzle perforated with many small holes through which a filament solution is forced. The filaments that emerge are solidified by cooling and the filaments twisted together to form a yarn.

SPINNING: The process of drawing out and twisting short fibers, for example, wool, and thus making a thread or yarn.

SPRING: A natural flow of water from the ground.

STABILIZER: A chemical that, when added to other chemicals, prevents further reactions. For example, in soda lime glass the lime acts as a stabilizer for the silica.

STAPLE: A short fiber that has to be twisted with other fibers (spun) in order to make a long thread or yarn

STARCHES: One form of carbohydrate. Starches can be used to make adhesives.

STATE OF MATTER: The physical form of matter. There are three states of matter: liquid, solid, and gas.

STEAM: Water vapor at the boiling point of water.

STONEWARE: Nonwhite pottery that has been fired at a high temperature until some of the clay has fused, a state called vitrified. Vitrification makes the pottery impervious to water. It is used for general tableware, often for breakfast crockery.

STRAND: When a number of yarns are twisted together, they make a strand. Strands twisted together make a rope.

SUBSTANCE: A type of material including mixtures.

SULFIDE: A compound that is composed only of metal and sulfur atoms, for example, PbS, the mineral galena.

SUPERCONDUCTORS: Materials that will conduct electricity with virtually no resistance if they are cooled to temperatures close to absolute zero ($-273°C$).

SURFACE TENSION: The force that operates on the surface of a liquid, and that makes it act as though it were covered with an invisible elastic film.

SURFACTANT: A substance that acts on a surface, such as a detergent.

SUSPENDED, SUSPENSION: Tiny particles in a liquid or a gas that do not settle out with time.

SYNTHETIC: Something that does not occur naturally but has to be manufactured. Synthetics are often produced from materials that do not occur in nature, for example, from petrochemicals. (i) Dye—a synthetic dye is made from petrochemicals, as opposed to natural dyes that are made of extracts of plants. (ii) Fiber—synthetic is a subdivision of artificial. Although both polyester and rayon are artificial fibers, rayon is made from reconstituted natural cellulose fibers and so is not synthetic, while polyester is made from petrochemicals and so is a synthetic fiber.

TANNIN: A group of pale-yellow or light-brown substances derived from plants that are used in dyeing fabric and making ink. Tannins are soluble in water and produce dark-blue or dark-green solutions when added to iron compounds.

TARNISH: A coating that develops as a result of the reaction between a metal and the substances in the air. The most common form of tarnishing is a very thin transparent oxide coating, such as occurs on aluminum. Sulfur compounds in the air make silver tarnish black.

TEMPER: To moderate or to make stronger: used in the metal industry to describe softening hardened steel or cast iron by reheating at a lower temperature or to describe hardening steel by reheating and cooling in oil; or in the glass industry, to describe toughening glass by first heating it and then slowly cooling it.

TEMPORARILY HARD WATER: Hard water that contains dissolved substances that can be removed by boiling.

TENSILE (PULLING STRENGTH): The greatest lengthwise (pulling) stress a substance can bear without tearing apart.

TENSION: A state of being pulled. Compare to compression.

TERRA COTTA: Red earth-colored glazed or unglazed fired clay whose origins lie in the Mediterranean region of Europe.

THERMOPLASTIC: A plastic that will soften and can be molded repeatedly into different shapes. It will then set into the molded shape as it cools.

THERMOSET: A plastic that will set into a molded shape as it first cools, but that cannot be made soft again by reheating.

THREAD: A long length of filament, group of filaments twisted together, or a long length of short fibers that have been spun and twisted together into a continuous strand.

TIMBER: A general term for wood suitable for building or for carpentry and consisting of roughcut planks.
Compare to **LUMBER**

TRANSITION METALS: Any of the group of metallic elements (for example, chromium and iron) that belong to the central part of the periodic table of the elements and whose oxides commonly occur in a variety of colors.

TRANSPARENT: Something that will readily let light through, for example, window glass. Compare to translucent, when only some light gets through but an image cannot be seen, for example, greaseproof paper.

TROPOSPHERE: The lower part of the atmosphere in which clouds form. In general, temperature decreases with height.

TRUNK: The main stem of a tree.

VACUUM: Something from which all air has been removed.

VAPOR: The gaseous phase of a substance that is a liquid or a solid at that temperature, for example, water vapor is the gaseous form of water.

VAPORIZE: To change from a liquid to a gas, or vapor.

VENEER: A thin sheet of highly decorative wood that is applied to cheap wood or engineered wood products to improve their appearance and value.

VINYL: Often used as a general name for plastic. Strictly, vinyls are polymers derived from ethylene by removal of one hydrogen atom, for example, PVC, polyvinylchloride.

VISCOSE: A yellow-brown solution made by treating cellulose with alkali solution and carbon disulfide and used to make rayon.

VISCOUS, VISCOSITY: Sticky. Viscosity is a measure of the resistance of a liquid to flow. The higher the viscosity— the more viscous it is—the less easily it will flow.

VITREOUS CHINA: A translucent form of china or porcelain.

VITRIFICATION: To heat until a substance changes into a glassy form and fuses together.

VOLATILE: Readily forms a gas. Some parts of a liquid mixture are often volatile, as is the case for crude oil. This allows them to be separated by distillation.

WATER CYCLE: The continual interchange of water between the oceans, the air, clouds, rain, rivers, ice sheets, soil, and rocks.

WATER VAPOR: The gaseous form of water.

WAVELENGTH: The distance between adjacent crests on a wave. Shorter wavelengths have smaller distances between crests than longer wavelengths.

WAX: Substances of animal, plant, mineral, or synthetic origin that are similar to fats but are less greasy and harder. They form hard films that can be polished.

WEAVING: A way of making a fabric by passing two sets of yarns through one another at right angles to make a kind of tight meshed net with no spaces between the yarns.

WELDING: Technique used for joining metal pieces through intense localized heat. Welding often involves the use of a joining metal such as a rod of steel used to attach steel pieces (arc welding).

WETTING: In adhesive spreading, a term that refers to the complete coverage of an adhesive over a surface.

WETTING AGENT: A substance that is able to cover a surface completely with a film of liquid. It is a substance with a very low surface tension.

WHITE GLASS: Also known as milk glass, it is an opaque white glass that was originally made in Venice and meant to look like porcelain.

WROUGHT IRON: A form of iron that is relatively soft and can be bent without breaking. It contains less than 0.1% carbon.

YARN: A strand of fibers twisted together and used to make textiles.

Set Index

USING THE SET INDEX

This index covers all nine volumes in the *Materials Science* set:

Volume
number   Title
- 1: Plastics
- 2: Metals
- 3: Wood and paper
- 4: Ceramics
- 5: Glass
- 6: Dyes, paints, and adhesives
- 7: Fibers
- 8: Water
- 9: Air

An example entry:
Index entries are listed alphabetically.

sinter, sintering **2:** 21; **4:** 9, 44

Volume numbers are in bold and are followed by page numbers.

In the example above, sinter, sintering appears in Volume 2: Metals on page 21 and in Volume 4: Ceramics on pages 9 and 44. Many terms also are covered in the Glossary on pages 58-64.

See or *see also* refers to another entry where there will be additional relevant information.

A

abrasive **4:** 6, 12
ABS. *See* acrylonitrile butadiene styrene
acetate fiber **6:** 21; **7:** 36, 46
acetate film **1:** 47
acetic acid **1:** 37, 55
acid rain **8:** 57; **9:** 21, 46, 47
acidic water **8:** 6, 7, 46, 48, 52, 57
acids **1:** 15; **2:** 28, 30; **8:** 6, 46, 47, 48, 52, 56, 57
acrylic **1:** 38, 39, 40, 41
acrylic adhesives **6:** 50
acrylic fiber **1:** 39; **6:** 20, 21; **7:** 33, 36, 37, 38, 44, 45, 57
acrylic paints and stains **1:** 41; **6:** 32, 34, 35
acrylic plastics **1:** 38-41
acrylic powders **6:** 40
acrylonitrile-butadiene-styrene (ABS) **1:** 38
addition polymers/addition polymerization **1:** 10, 11, 27, 43; **7:** 15
additives **1:** 15, 16, 17; **3:** 51
adhesion **6:** 44, 45, 46
adhesives **1:** 22, 37, 40, 41, 42, 44, 53, 55; **3:** 8, 24, 43, 44, 45, 47, 50, 53, 54; **4:** 35, 41; **5:** 54; **6:** 4, 41-57

adhesive tapes **6:** 54, 57
admiralty brass **2:** 24
adobe **4:** 10, 11
advanced ceramics **4:** 42-57
aggregate **4:** 39, 41
air **9:** 4 AND THROUGHOUT
air bags **9:** 42
air brakes **9:** 35
air conditioning **9:** 26, 52
aircraft **2:** 21, 26, 27, 35, 51; **9:** 29, 32, 34, 35
air cushions **9:** 34-35
air drying **3:** 36
air gun **9:** 35
air in transportation **9:** 32
air pollution **9:** 19, 38-40, 44, 46-47
air pressure **9:** 5, 6, 28, 32, 37
albumen **6:** 49
alcohols **8:** 45, 51
alizarin **6:** 12, 13, 14
alkalis **1:** 15; **2:** 28, 30; **8:** 52
alkyd-based paint **6:** 31, 33
alkyd-based varnishes **6:** 37
alloys, alloying **1:** 15; **2:** 6, 13, 22, 23-27, 28, 34, 35, 37, 42; **4:** 46
alum **3:** 53; **6:** 10
alumina **4:** 38, 46, 50, 51, 54, 56, 57; **5:** 8, 9, 10, 13, 18, 52
aluminosilicates **4:** 14
aluminum **2:** 4, 5, 9, 10, 18, 19, 20, 21, 23, 24, 26, 27, 29, 30, 32, 50, 53; **4:** 14, 36
aluminum oxide **4:** 46, 50, 57; **5:** 13
amethyst **4:** 33
amides **7:** 10, 47
ammonia **9:** 41
amorphous solid **5:** 5, 15
amphibious vehicles **9:** 33
anaerobics **6:** 50
ancient glass **5:** 29
angle of incidence **5:** 20
aniline dyes **6:** 14, 22; **7:** 38
aniline mauve **6:** 14
animal glue **6:** 49
anions **8:** 10
annealing **5:** 50
anodized aluminum **2:** 32
anodizing **2:** 27, 32
antimony **2:** 45
antirust paint **6:** 33
anvil **2:** 12, 20
aqueous solutions **8:** 43, 44, 46
Araldite® **1:** 55
aramids **7:** 36, 50, 51
Archimedes' principle **8:** 38
argon **9:** 18, 36, 54, 55
armor **2:** 42, 43
armor plating **2:** 42
Arnel® **1:** 47; **7:** 46
arsenic oxide **5:** 11
artifacts **4:** 12
artificial dyes **6:** 7
artificial fibers **3:** 50; **7:** 7, 8, 9, 10, 12, 15, 16, 17, 19, 24, 30, 31, 32-57
artificial polymers **7:** 12
aspen **3:** 15
atmosphere **9:** 12, 14, 18, 20-21, 43, 44, 54, 55
atmospheric pressure **8:** 21, 22, 28; **9:** 6. *See also* air pressure
atomizer **9:** 28

atoms **2:** 6, 8, 9, 22, 23; **4:** 5, 9; **5:** 4, 5, 39; **7:** 4, 9; **8:** 8; **9:** 8, 10
atoms, properties in plastics **1:** 13
ax **3:** 6
azo dyes and pigments **6:** 7, 10; **7:** 38

B

backbone chain **1:** 27, 43, 55; **7:** 4. *See also* polymers
backbone unit **1:** 54. *See also* monomers
bagasse **3:** 49
Bakelite **1:** 43
balloons **9:** 8, 14, 51, 54
balsa **3:** 17, 20, 23
bamboo **3:** 49
band saw **3:** 34
barbed wire **2:** 6, 30, 31
barium carbonate **4:** 46; **5:** 9
barium titanate **4:** 46
bark **3:** 4, 6, 13, 14, 32
barometer **8:** 28
base metal **2:** 23, 24
bast fibers **7:** 20
batch kiln **4:** 19, 28
batch processing **7:** 32
batik **6:** 19
bauxite **4:** 38
beating metals **2:** 22-23
beech **3:** 17, 18, 23
bellows **9:** 28
bells **2:** 14, 44
bending ceramics **4:** 9
bending metals **2:** 12, 22, 23, 31, 34
bends, the **8:** 41
benzene **1:** 33, 39
benzene ring **1:** 10; **6:** 15
Bessemer converter **2:** 46
Bessemer, Henry **2:** 47
binder **4:** 55; **6:** 27, 39
bioceramics **4:** 54-56
blacksmith **2:** 12, 22, 41
blast furnace **2:** 47
bleaches **6:** 24, 26
bleaching paper **3:** 52, 57
blending fibers **7:** 12, 25, 41, 43, 44, 45
blending, blending ceramics **4:** 17, 22, 26, 28
blood **8:** 8, 48
blood glue **6:** 49
bloom **2:** 40
blow molding **1:** 19
blown glass **5:** 32-33
board **3:** 34, 36, 42, 43, 44, 45, 46
bobbin **7:** 25, 42
boil, boiling water **8:** 11, 16, 20, 48
boilers **8:** 21, 22, 32, 33, 54
boiling point of water **11, 19, 20, 49, 48, 54
boll, boll fiber **7:** 4, 20, 25
bond paper **3:** 55
bonds and bonding **2:** 6, 7; **4:** 4, 5, 6, 9, 15, 25; **8:** 8, 9, 11, 14. *See also* covalent bonding, hydrogen bonds and bonding, ionic bonding
bone china **4:** 25
book paper **3:** 55
borax **5:** 13
boric oxide **5:** 8, 13
borosilicate glass **5:** 12, 13, 19
bottles **5:** 10, 28, 30, 43, 46-47
Boyle's law **9:** 8, 9
brass **2:** 6, 16, 24, 34, 41, 44

65

brazilwood **6:** 12
brick **8:** 26, 27, 28
brick colors **4:** 15, 16, 27, 29
bricks and brick making **4:** 4, 10, 14, 15, 16, 17, 19, 26-31, 32, 33, 34, 39
brighteners, for fabric and paper **6:** 24
brine **8:** 41, 47, 50, 51
bristles **7:** 6, 48
brittleness in materials **2:** 4, 8, 14, 17, 18, 41; **3:** 19; **4:** 4, 8-9; **5:** 5, 23
broad-leaved trees **3:** 17
bronze **2:** 15, 25, 37, 38, 39, 40, 41, 43, 44, 45, 55
Bronze Age **2:** 14, 37-38, 40, 41, 55
buildings, use of metals in **2:** 18, 28, 31, 49, 54-57
bull's-eye glass **5:** 39
bulletproof glass **5:** 26
bulletproof vests **7:** 8, 14, 34, 51
bullets **2:** 42, 45
buoyancy **8:** 38-39
burlap **7:** 11
burn **3:** 27, 28
burning plastics **1:** 12, 13, 14, 25
butadiene rubber **1:** 42
butene **1:** 28

C

cadmium **2:** 10, 30
calcium **2:** 5, 10; **4:** 15, 36, 53
calcium halophosphate **4:** 52
calcium oxide **4:** 37, 38; **5:** 8
calcium silicate **4:** 52
calcium sulfate **4:** 34
calcium tungstate **4:** 52
calorific value of wood **3:** 28
cambium **3:** 10, 12, 13, 14
cannons **2:** 15, 25, 44, 45
canoes **1:** 53; **3:** 6
canvas **7:** 11
capacitors **4:** 7, 44, 46-47; **5:** 18
capillarity **8:** 26-28
capillary action **6:** 54
car industry **2:** 49, 52
carbohydrates **7:** 10
carbon **1:** 4, 6, 7, 10, 13, 16, 27, 38, 39, 41, 42, 43, 54, 55, 57; **2:** 10, 23, 39, 41; **4:** 6; **7:** 4, 7, 8, 14, 49, 50, 53, 55, 56; **9:** 21, 48, 49
carbon black **1:** 42; **6:** 9, 29
carbon chains **1:** 7, 13, 27
carbon compounds **1:** 4; **6:** 9
carbon cycle **9:** 48, 49
carbon dioxide **9:** 11, 19, 36, 43, 48-50, 51
carbon fiber **4:** 57; **7:** 56-57
carbonic acid **8:** 48
cardboard **3:** 46, 56
carding **7:** 25
carmine **6:** 12, 13, 14
carpets **7:** 24, 25, 27, 33, 43, 44, 45, 48, 49
carving **3:** 9, 22
casein **6:** 49
cashmere **7:** 27
cassiterite **2:** 38
cast bronze **2:** 15, 45
cast glass **5:** 30
casting **2:** 13, 14, 17, 18, 25, 38, 39, 44; **4:** 17, 18, 43
cast iron **2:** 40, 41, 45, 49, 54, 55, 56, 57
catalysts **7:** 15, 42; **8:** 7; **9:** 10, 41

catalytic converters **2:** 11; **4:** 43, 53, 57; **9:** 39, 40
cations **4:** 6, 15; **8:** 10
cedar **3:** 16
Celanese® **7:** 46
cellophane **1:** 47
cells **3:** 10-3, 14, 18, 22, 23, 27, 28
celluloid **1:** 7, 46
cellulose **1:** 14, 46, 47, 49; **3:** 10, 46, 47, 48, 50, 51, 52; **7:** 10, 11, 12, 13, 25, 31, 39, 40, 41, 46
cellulose diacetate **1:** 47
cement **4:** 10, 13, 33-37, 38, 39, 40, 41. *See also* dental cement
central heating systems **2:** 56; **8:** 32, 33; **9:** 25, 26, 27
ceramic **4:** 4 AND THROUGHOUT
ceramic capacitors **4:** 46-47
ceramic electrical insulators **3:** 28; **9:** 22
ceramic molds **1:** 9
ceramics **1:** 15, 16; **2:** 4, 12, 49; **5:** 4, 5, 14
ceramics used in nuclear reactors **4:** 54
ceramic tiles. *See* tiles
CFCs. *See* chlorofluorocarbons
chain mail **2:** 42
chalcogenide glasses **5:** 15
change of state **8:** 5, 16-20, 21, 22; **9:** 52
charcoal **2:** 38, 39, 40, 41, 46, 47
Charles's law **9:** 9
charring **7:** 7, 10, 15, 17, 24, 33, 39, 44, 57
checks **3:** 20
chemical properties of glass **5:** 16-18
chewing gum **1:** 8
chicle **1:** 8
china **4:** 25
china clay **3:** 51, 54; **4:** 14, 16, 24, 25; **6:** 9
chipboard, chipwood **1:** 22; **3:** 34, 42, 43, 44
chips, chippings **3:** 11, 32, 34, 50
chlorine **1:** 10, 29, 39; **3:** 52
chloroethylene **1:** 10
chlorofluorocarbons (CFCs) **9:** 44
chromium **2:** 10, 25, 28, 30; **5:** 11, 21
chromium plating **2:** 30, 34
circular saw **3:** 34
clay minerals **4:** 14
clays **4:** 4, 9, 10, 14, 15, 17, 18, 28
clay suspensions **4:** 17, 18
clearcut tree felling **3:** 32
cling wrap **1:** 11
clothing **7:** 8, 16, 29, 33, 39, 41, 43, 44, 45
clouds and cloud formation **8:** 4, 7; **9:** 3, 9, 20, 52, 53
coal **2:** 47, 49; **9:** 48, 49
coal tar **6:** 7, 8, 10, 16
coated papers **3:** 55
cobalt **2:** 9; **5:** 11, 21
cobalt aluminate **4:** 51
cobalt oxide **5:** 11
cobalt silicate **4:** 51
cochineal **6:** 12, 13
coins **2:** 20, 26, 38, 39
coir **7:** 11
coke **2:** 47
cold bending **2:** 35
cold forging **2:** 20, 23
cold rolling **2:** 18
cold-working metals **2:** 14
collecting gases **9:** 10
colorants **1:** 15, 16; **6:** 6, 9, 10, 24, 25, 26

colored glass **5:** 21, 33-35
colorfast **6:** 8; **7:** 52
coloring glass **5:** 11
coloring paper **3:** 54
color mixing **6:** 4-6
composite materials **7:** 56, 57
composite wood **3:** 24
compounds of metals **2:** 4, 6; **9:** 36, 38, 43, 47, 48
compressed air **9:** 11, 28, 31, 34, 35, 54
compressibility of water **8:** 31
compression molding **1:** 18
compression resistance in ceramics **4:** 8
concrete **4:** 10, 35, 39-41
condensation **8:** 16, 18-19, 49, 50; **9:** 16, 53
condensation polymer, condensation polymerization **1:** 43; **7:** 10, 14
conductivity. *See* electrical conductivity and heat (thermal) conductivity
conifers, coniferous trees **3:** 16, 48
contact adhesives **6:** 41, 52-53
contact lenses **1:** 40
continuous casting **2:** 17
continuous production tunnel kilns **4:** 30
convection **9:** 18, 22, 25, 27. *See also* heat convection
cooling towers **8:** 34
copolymer **1:** 38
copper **2:** 4, 5, 6, 9, 10, 14, 16, 17, 23, 24, 25, 26, 27, 28, 30, 36, 37, 38, 39, 40, 41, 43, 45, 53, 56; **4:** 47; **5:** 11
copper ore **2:** 5
copper oxide **5:** 11
cores **5:** 30, 31
corn glue **6:** 49
Corning Corporation **5:** 13
corrosion **2:** 28, 32; **8:** 27, 53, 54, 57
corrosion in glass **5:** 13, 14, 16, 17, 18
corrosion in water **8:** 53-54
corrosion resistance **1:** 29, 30, 43; **2:** 23, 24, 25, 26, 27, 28-34, 38, 49, 51; **4:** 32, 46, 54, 55, 57
corrugated iron **2:** 31
cotton **1:** 13, 51; **3:** 49, 55; **7:** 4, 7, 17, 19, 20, 21, 25, 43
covalent bonding **4:** 5; **8:** 8, 9
crankshaft **8:** 22
crease-resistant fabrics **7:** 17, 27, 42, 46. *See also* durable-, permanent-, and stay-pressed fabrics
creosote **3:** 24, 40; **6:** 36
creping **3:** 56
crimped materials **7:** 27, 37; **8:** 26
cristallo **5:** 37
critical angle **5:** 20
crockery **4:** 19, 24
cross linking **7:** 17
crown glass **5:** 39, 49
crucible glass **5:** 29-30
crucibles **2:** 47; **4:** 32
crude oil **1:** 6, 28; **6:** 7, 8, 10, 16, 26, 36; **9:** 45
crysocolla **2:** 5
crystal glass **5:** 37
Crystal Palace **2:** 56; **5:** 42
crystals and crystalline materials **2:** 3, 6, 13, 14, 18, 22; **4:** 6-8, 9, 19, 34, 35, 39, 43, 48, 50, 52, 5, 4, 6, 14
cullet **5:** 42
curing concrete **4:** 39

curing rubber **1**: 9
cut glass **5**: 9
cutlery **2**: 31
cyanoacrylate **1**: 40; **6**: 50, 54
cylinder glass **5**: 40
cylinders **8**: 21, 22

D

Dacron® **1**: 50; **7**: 42
daggers **2**: 41
Dalton, John **9**: 11
Dalton's law **9**: 10
Damascus steel **2**: 41
damp-proof layer **8**: 28
Darby, Abraham 47
debarking machine **3**: 34
decay in wood **3**: 24, 30, 41, 43
deciduous trees **3**: 30
decolorizing glass **5**: 11, 36
decompose **7**: 7, 10, 14, 24, 33, 44
decomposition of plastics **1**: 24, 49
decomposition of water **8**: 17, 56
decompression sickness **9**: 42
decorative laminates **1**: 22
defibering **3**: 53
density of gases **9**: 9, 15
density of plastics **1**: 4, 24, 29, 32, 33
density of water **8**: 8, 12, 13, 20, 28, 31, 37, 39
density of wood **3**: 20-24, 27
dental cement **4**: 55-56
dental fillings **4**: 3, 55
desalination **8**: 41, 50-51
desalting **8**: 41. See also desalination
detergents **8**: 11, 10-41, 48, 55
deuterium **8**: 14
diamond **4**: 4, 6, 57
die casting **2**: 17
die extrusion **1**: 17, 18, **2**: 19
diene plastics **1**: 42, 43
dies **2**: 17, 19, 21, 39; **4**: 17, 28, 57
diffusion **8**: 39, 40; **9**: 17
dipping **1**: 21
direct dyeing **7**: 30
dishwasher-proof plastic containers **1**: 32
disperse dyeing **6**: 21-22
disposable plastics **1**: 14, 20, 23, 24, 33, 17, 51
dissociation in water **8**: 16, 47, 55(gloss)
dissolving substances in water **8**: 6, 42-57
distillation of air **9**: 36
distillation of water **8**: 49-51
distilled water **8**: 49, 50
doped ceramics **4**: 8, 45, 51, 52, 53
doping **4**: 6, 45
double glazing **5**: 26; **9**: 23
Douglas fir **3**: 16, 20
drafts **9**: 27
drawing **2**: 13, 19
drawing dies **2**: 19; **4**: 57
drawing fibers. See stretching fibers
drinking water supplies **8**: 6
drip-dry fabrics **1**: 47
dry cleaned **7**: 41
dry felting **3**: 45
dry ice **9**: 50
drying wood **3**: 23, 36, 37
dry-press process **4**: 28
dry spinning **7**: 34
ductile material **2**: 18
Dumas, Jean-Baptiste-André **5**: 38

durable-press fabrics **7**: 16-17. See also permanent- and stay-pressed fabrics
dyeing artificial fibers **7**: 37
dyeing metals **2**: 32
dyeing natural fibers **6**: 7, 17, 18, 20, 21, 24; **7**: 30
dyeing plastics **1**: 16, 39
dyeing synthetic fibers **6**: 17, 20, 21
dyes **6**: 4-26; **7**: 7, 30, 38
dyes and dyeing fibers **6**: 6, 7, 17, 21, 22, 23, 24; **7**: 7, 24, 25, 27, 29, 30, 37, 38, 41, 42, 45, 46, 47, 51, 52
dyes and papermaking **3**: 51, 54

E

early wood **3**: 14
earthenware **4**: 22, 23, 24, 25
eggshell paint **6**: 34
Egypt **5**: 28, 33
Egyptians **5**: 30
Eiffel Tower **2**: 54
eighteen-carat gold **2**: 26
elastic limit **2**: 20, 35
elasticity in materials **1**: 8, 56, 57; **2**: 20, 22, 35; **5**: 23; **7**: 4, 7, 37, 47, 57; **9**: 14, 28
elastic properties of wood **3**: 8, 19, 29
electrical conductivity **1**: 4, 13, 14; **2**: 4, 6, 9, 11, 25, 53; **4**: 4, 6, 7, 8, 45, 46, 52-53, 56; **5**: 15, 18; **7**: 56, 57; **8**: 10, 44, 46-48; **9**: 21, 22
electrical insulation **1**: 13, 14, 29, 32, 35, 37, 44, 49; **3**: 28; **4**: 7, 22, 44, 46, 52, 56; **5**: 18; **8**: 46, 47; **9**: 21, 22
electrical properties of glass **5**: 18
electrical transformers **1**: 10
electric arc furnace **2**: 49
electric arc welding **2**: 52
electrofloat process **5**: 50
electrolysis **8**: 47, 56
electrolytes **8**: 46, 48
electromagnet **2**: 9
electronics **4**: 44-45, 46, 52, 53
electrons **1**: 13; **2**: 6, 7, 9, 28, 30; **4**: 5, 7, 47, 52; **8**: 9, 47, 56
elements **2**: 4, 8; **8**: 4; **9**: 4. See also heating elements
Empire State Building **2**: 57
emulsion paints **6**: 33, 34
enamel paints **2**: 33; **6**: 38
enamels, enameling **2**: 24, 33, 49, 57; **4**: 23; **5**: 14; **6**: 38
energy **8**: 14, 16, 17, 23, 35
energy efficient glasses **5**: 15
engineered wood products **3**: 42
epoxy, epoxy resin **1**: 53, 54, 55
epoxy resin adhesives **6**: 50-51
epoxy resin varnishes **6**: 37
etching glass **5**: 17
ethylene **1**: 10, 17, 20, 28, 33, 35, 37, 41
ethylene-propylene **1**: 32
eucalyptus **3**: 15
evaporation **8**: 4, 6, 16, 18-19, 20, 42
exosphere **9**: 20
exothermic reaction **8**: 52
expansion properties of glass **5**: 19
external combustion engine **8**: 22
extrusion **1**: 17, 19; **2**: 13, 19; **7**: 4, 10, 14, 32, 33, 34, 36, 37, 38, 42, 45, 46
eyeglasses **1**: 20; **5**: 26, 55

F

fabrics **1**: 13, 31, 44, 45, 47; **7**: 8, 10, 12, 15, 19, 20, 22, 25, 33
fat **8**: 30, 45, 46, 52
feldspars **4**: 15, 17, 22, 26, 29
felt **3**: 51
felting **3**: 45, 46; **7**: 28
ferric oxide **5**: 11
ferrites **4**: 48, 49
ferromagnetic metals **2**: 10
ferrous oxide **5**: 11
fertilizers **8**: 6; **9**: 36, 38, 41
fiberboard **3**: 45
fiberglass **1**: 16, 23; **2**: 12; **5**: 54, 57; **7**: 6, 54; **9**: 23. See also glass fiber
fibers **1**: 7, 18, 23, 25, 31, 39, 44, 46, 47, 48, 50, 51, 56; **3**: 4, 18, 22, 23, 24, 26, 28, 45, 46; **6**: 6, 17, 22, 23, 24; **7**: 4 AND THROUGHOUT; **9**: 23, 52
fibers in papermaking **3**: 4, 46-57
fibrin **7**: 28
filaments **6**: 41; **7**: 4, 28, 32, 33, 34, 47
filler **5**: 54; **4**: 15, 29, 30, 33, 39, 55; **6**: 9
finishes on paper **3**: 53-54
fir **3**: 16, 20
fire extinguishers **8**: 36, 37; **9**: 50
fire resistance **1**: 12, 14, 38, 46, 48, 52; **7**: 8, 14, 34, 45, 54
firing bricks **4**: 28-29, 30-31
firing ceramics **4**: 18-19, 20, 28, 29, 30, 31, 46
firing temperature **4**: 20, 30
fishing line **1**: 48, 49; **7**: 49, 54
flak jacket **2**: 42
flame resistance in wood **3**: 19
flash distillation **8**: 50-51
flat glass **5**: 33, 34, 39, 40, 42, 49-52, 53
flat paint **6**: 34
flax **3**: 49; **7**: 19, 20, 21
fleece **7**: 26
flexibility in fibers **7**: 6, 7
flint **4**: 5
float glass **5**: 49, 50, 51
float glass process **5**: 50-51
floating **8**: 8, 38-39, 51
fluorescent lamps and tubes **4**: 51, 57; **9**: 55, 56
fluorine **1**: 10, 41
fluorite **4**: 50
fluxes **2**: 40; **4**: 15, 16, 27, 29; **5**: 8, 9, 16
foamed polystyrene **1**: 14, 23, 32, 34
foaming agents **1**: 21; **8**: 37
foams and foamed plastics **1**: 14, 21-22, 23, 32, 33, 34, 56, 57
food coloring **6**: 24, 25-26
forests **3**: 10, 17, 30, 31, 32, 56
forging **2**: 13, 20, 23 41
former **5**: 8
Formica® **1**: 44
forming bricks **4**: 17, 28, 29
fossil fuels **9**: 38, 47, 48, 49
fractional distillation **9**: 36
fracturing in ceramics **4**: 5, 8, 9
fracturing in glass **5**: 6, 12, 13, 24
frame for construction **3**: 5, 7, 38, 44
freeze-dried ceramics **4**: 43
freeze-dry food **9**: 41
freezing **8**: 16, 17
freezing point of water **8**: 8, 31, 49, 50
fresh water **8**: 6
frit **5**: 52; **6**: 39

froth flotation **8:** 51
froth separation **8:** 51
fuel, wood **3:** 5, 6, 28
fumes **1:** 14, 25
furnaces **2:** 12, 41. *See also* glass furnaces
furniture **1:** 14, 22; **3:** 5, 17, 19, 22, 32, 36, 42, 43
fuses **2:** 26
fusing ceramics **4:** 9, 19, 20, 24, 30

G

galvanic protection **2:** 30-32
galvanized iron **2:** 57
galvanized steel **1:** 13;l **2:** 30, 31
galvanizing **2:** 6, 31
gang saw **3:** 34
gaseous state of water. *See* water vapor
gases **8:** 4, 5, 6, 7, 16, 17, 24, 42, 47, 56, 57; **9:** 4 AND THROUGHOUT
gas laws **9:** 8-10
gas-proof plastics **1:** 37, 51
gears **2:** 21
gelatin **6:** 48
gel spinning **7:** 34, 36
giant molecules **7:** 4
gilding metals **2:** 24
ginning **7:** 25
glass **1:** 12, 13, 23, 38, 40, 44, 52; **2:** 4, 33, 50, 56; **4:** 4, 9, 19, 20, 21, 22, 25, 26, 30, 32, 40; **5:** 4 AND THROUGHOUT; **6:** 38
glass adhesives **6:** 55
glass beads **6:** 39
glass blowing **5:** 33
glass ceramics **4:** 53; **5:** 14, 19
glass enamel **2:** 33; **6:** 38
glass fiber **1:** 16, 22, 23, 53; **4:** 57; **7:** 6, 53-54, 55, 56; **5:** 13, 54
glass furnaces **5:** 14, 29, 32, 36, 41, 42, 43, 50, 55
glassmaker's soap **5:** 36
glass microfiber **7:** 6
glass powder **6:** 38, 39
glass transition temperature **7:** 44
glassy state **5:** 5
glazes and glazing **4:** 9, 20-21, 22, 23, 24, 25, 29, 31, 51; **5:** 13, 14, 24; **6:** 38
global warming **9:** 49
gloss paint **6:** 29, 31, 33, 34, 35
glucose **3:** 10; **7:** 12
glue **6:** 10, 41, 48-49
glulam **3:** 42
gobs **5:** 32, 43
gold **2:** 4, 5, 9, 10, 11, 25, 26, 28, 36, 37, 39, 40; **8:** 55
Golden Gate Bridge **2:** 56-57
gold nuggets **2:** 36, 37
Goop **6:** 56
grain, in wood **3:** 9, 16, 17, 18, 24
graphite **4:** 4, 6, 7, 57
gravity **8:** 25, 32; **9:** 14
greaseproof paper **3:** 56
Greece **5:** 28
Greeks **2:** 42, 43; **4:** 13, 35; **8:** 4
greenhouse effect **9:** 21, 49, 50
ground glass **5:** 17, 36, 49, 56
groundwater **8:** 7, 55
growth rings **3:** 13, 14, 16, 20
gum arabic **6:** 49
gums **3:** 10, 12, 13, 14, 20, 22, 27, 46, 54; **6:** 49; **7:** 19, 20

gunmetal **2:** 25
gypsum **4:** 34, 37, 38

H

hairs **7:** 6, 7, 9, 10, 21, 22, 25, 26, 27
Hall, Charles M. **2:** 50
hammering metals **2:** 20, 37, 39, 40, 41, 43
hard water **8:** 55
hardness in metals **2:** 8
hardwoods **3:** 16, 17, 18, 19, 22, 23, 28, 48
harvesting trees **3:** 30-32
HDPE. *See* high-density polyethylene
headsaw **3:** 34, 36
heartwood **3:** 12, 13, 14
heat—effect on plastics **1:** 4, 11, 12, 13, 14, 21, 24, 25, 35, 37, 43, 44, 48, 52
heating elements **4:** 52, 53; **8:** 38, 55
heating metals **2:** 12, 13, 20, 21, 22-23, 26, 40, 41
heat (thermal) conductivity **1:** 14; **2:** 4, 6, 9, 33; **4:** 4; **5:** 7, 12, 19; **8:** 32-35, 37; **9:** 15, 22, 26, 27
heat (thermal) insulation **1:** 14, 21, 23, 34, 43, 53, 57; **3:** 8, 27-28, 57; **4:** 42; **5:** 7, 18; **7:** 27, 36, 46, 54; **9:** 22-23
heat capacity **8:** 32. *See also* thermal capacity
heat convection **8:** 37-38; **9:** 25, 27
heat storage **8:** 32-35
heavy water **8:** 14, 15
helium **9:** 18, 54-55
hematite **2:** 5
hemp **7:** 11, 19, 20, 21
Héroult, Paul-Louis-Toussaint **2:** 50
high-density polyethylene (HDPE) **1:** 26, 29, 30, 31, 32
high-k glass **5:** 18
Hindenburg **9:** 51
holograms **5:** 22
hot glue **1:** 42
hot rolling **2:** 18
hotworking **2:** 13, 14
household water systems **8:** 33
hovercrafts **9:** 32-34
human hair **7:** 6
humidity **9:** 21, 26, 52, 53
hydration **4:** 35; **8:** 56
hydraulics and hydraulic action **8:** 31
hydroelectric power generation **8:** 35
hydrofluoric acid etching **5:** 17
hydrogen **8:** 8, 9, 14, 16, 47, 52, 54, 55-56; **9:** 10, 18, 19, 41, 49, 51, 54
hydrogen bonds and bonding **6:** 20; **7:** 17, 39, 51; **8:** 11-13, 14, 36
hydrogen chloride **1:** 35
hydrolysis **7:** 46
hydrophilic substances **8:** 30, 45
hydrophobic substances **8:** 29, 30, 45
hygrometer **9:** 52
hypocaust **9:** 24, 25

I

ice **8:** 8, 11, 12, 13, 16, 17, 24, 25
Illing, Moritz **3:** 53
immiscibility **8:** 28
impermeable ceramics **4:** 20, 22. *See also* watertight ceramics
impurities in water **8:** 7, 48, 49
indigo **6:** 11, 13, 14, 15, 20, 21
indium oxide **4:** 53

Industrial Revolution **2:** 43, 46-49, 54; **4:** 13; **7:** 22; **8:** 21
inert gases **9:** 21, 41, 42, 53, 55
ingrain dyeing **6:** 21, 22; **7:** 38
injection molding **1:** 18, 25, 32, 50
inks **6:** 8, 9
inner bark **3:** 12, 13
inorganic materials **6:** 9
insulation. *See* electrical insulation and heat (thermal) insulation
integrated circuits **4:** 8, 45
International Space Station **5:** 52
ionic bonding **4:** 5
ionic substances **8:** 42, 46
ions **2:** 6, 7; **4:** 6, 7, 8, 15; **8:** 9, 40, 41, 42, 43, 44, 46, 47
iron **2:** 4, 5, 9, 10, 11, 12, 16, 18, 21, 22, 23, 25, 30, 31, 37, 38, 39, 40, 41, 43, 44, 45, 46, 47, 49, 54, 55, 560, 41, 43, 46, 47; **4:** 16, 24, 27, 36, 38, 48; **8:** 53, 54
Iron Age **2:** 38-41
ironed **7:** 33
ironing fibers **7:** 16-17, 33, 41, 44, 49
ironwood **3:** 20
iron ore **2:** 5
iron oxide **2:** 5, 40; **4:** 38, 49; **5:** 8
iron staining **4:** 16, 24, 27
irrigation **8:** 6
isocyanates **6:** 43
isoprene **1:** 6, 8
isotopes **8:** 14
ivory **1:** 46

J

Jesse Littleton **5:** 13
jewelry **2:** 24, 25, 26, 36, 37, 39, 50
jiggering **4:** 25
jute **7:** 19, 20

K

kaolin, kaolinite **3:** 54; **4:** 14, 16, 24, 25
kapok **7:** 20
keratin **7:** 26
Kevlar® **1:** 48; **2:** 42; **7:** 8, 34, 50, 51
kiln drying of wood **3:** 36, 37
kilns **4:** 9, 19, 27, 32, 35, 37, 38, 51; **5:** 14, 38
kinetic energy **8:** 35
knapping **5:** 7
knitting **7:** 22, 23
knots **3:** 18, 20, 26
kraft process **3:** 51, 52
krypton **9:** 18, 54, 56

L

lacquers **1:** 11, 53; **2:** 29; **6:** 40, 42
laminated glass **5:** 21, 26, 27, 28
laminated windshields and safety glass **1:** 23, 37, 37
laminates **1:** 22, 23, 44; **3:** 24 **6:** 50
lanolin **7:** 26
lasers **4:** 52; **5:** 57
latent heat **8:** 17
latent heat **9:** 16, 52
late wood **3:** 14
latex **1:** 8; **3:** 54; **6:** 29, 49
latex paints **6:** 29, 34, 35
lathed glass **5:** 30
lattice **8:** 12, 17
laundry powder **6:** 3, 24

LCDs. *See* liquid crystal displays
LDPE. *See* low-density polyethylene
lead **2:** 10, 11, 24, 25, 40, 42, 43, 44
lead crystal glass **5:** 37
lead monoxide **5:** 11
lead oxide **4:** 53; **5:** 8, 11
lead-silicate glass **5:** 22, 55
leaf fiber **7:** 19
leather **6:** 17
lenses **4:** 50; **5:** 9, 21, 22, 26, 55, 56
Liberty Bell **2:** 14
lift, using air **9:** 32, 34, 35
light bulb filaments **2:** 9, 21, 53
light bulbs **5:** 13, 43, 44-45
lightfast pigments **6:** 9
lignin **3:** 10, 46, 48, 50, 51
lime **4:** 13, 35, 38; **5:** 8, 9, 10, 13, 16, 17, 18, 22, 29, 30, 38
limestone **4:** 35, 36, 37, 38; **5:** 9, 38
linen, linen fibers **3:** 49; **7:** 20, 21
linseed oil **1:** 52; **6:** 30, 37
liquefying gases **9:** 14, 36, 41
liquid crystal displays (LCDs) **4:** 53
liquid oxygen **9:** 36
liquid state of water **8:** 8, 15, 16, 19, 20, 21
liquids **5:** 5; **9:** 5, 12; **8:** 4, 5, 14, 16, 17, 19
lithium **2:** 27, 53
lithium oxide **5:** 9
lodestone **4:** 48
logs **3:** 5, 8, 23, 30, 31, 32, 34, 35, 36, 42
logwood **6:** 12
low-density polyethylene (LDPE) **1:** 26, 27, 28, 29, 30
lubricant **4:** 6, 7, 57
lumber **3:** 33
Lyrca® **7:** 52

M

machinability of metal alloys **2:** 23
machine-made glass **5:** 42-57
madder plant **6:** 12, 13
magnesia **5:** 8, 9
magnesium **2:** 5, 10, 25, 26, 27, 32, 50
magnetic ceramics **4:** 48-49
magnetic properties of glass **5:** 15
magnetism in ceramics **4:** 48-49
magnesium in metals **2:** 9-10
magnetite **2:** 9; **4:** 48
magnets **4:** 44, 48
mandrel **5:** 53
manganese **5:** 11, 21
man-made fibers **7:** 12, 31
maple **3:** 27
marine ply **3:** 43
Martin, Pierre and Émile **2:** 47
massicot **6:** 12
matting of fibers **7:** 21, 28
mechanical properties of glass **5:** 22-24
medicines **8:** 48
melamine **1:** 22, 45, 53; **6:** 29, 40
melamine-formaldehyde **1:** 22
melting **8:** 8, 11, 12, 14, 16, 17, 49
melting point of water **8:** 11, 49
melting points of metals **2:** 6
melt spinning **7:** 34, 36
mercuric oxide decomposition **9:** 12
mercury **2:** 10, 43
mesosphere **9:** 20
metal fatigue **2:** 27, 35
metallic glasses **5:** 15

metalloids **2:** 8
metal ores **2:** 5, 9, 37, 38
metal oxides **4:** 20, 27, 48; **5:** 11
metallurgy **2:** 12
metals **1:** 4, 5, 12, 13, 15, 16, 23, 48, 52, 55, 56, 57; **2:** 4 AND THROUGHOUT; **3:** 6, 8, 26; **4:** 4, 7, 8, 9, 16, 30, 46, 48, 51, 56; **5:** 6, 15; **8:** 53-55
methane **9:** 18
methyl orange **6:** 14
microelectronic circuits **4:** 53
microfiber **5:** 57; **7:** 6, 18, 19, 46
Middle Ages **2:** 39, 43, 44
mild steel **2:** 29, 49
milk glue **6:** 49
millefiori **5:** 33
minerals **4:** 4, 34, 50; **5:** 4. *See also* clay minerals
mineral water **8:** 7
mining **2:** 5
minting **2:** 39
mirrors **5:** 22, 56
mixtures and water **8:** 19, 32, 42, 49
mixtures in metals **2:** 6, 23
mixtures, mixture of gases **9:** 4, 10, 16-17
modacrylic **7:** 36
moderator **8:** 14
moisture in the atmosphere **9:** 52-53
mold, molding **1:** 9, 12, 18, 19, 20, 21
molded glass **5:** 30
molds and molding **2:** 14, 15, 16, 17, 39, 41; **4:** 9, 12, 17, 28, 29, 43; **5:** 30, 43, 44, 46, 49, 54, 55
molecules **8:** 8, 24. *See also* water molecules
molecules and molecular structures **1:** 6, 7, 10, 11, 33; **7:** 4, 8, 9, 10, 12, 13, 14, 17, 30, 32, 34, 37, 44; **9:** 7, 8, 9, 12-14, 15, 16, 17, 18, 37, 44, 53
monomers **1:** 10
mordant **3:** 53; **6:** 7, 10, 12, 20; **7:** 30
mortar **4:** 16, 35, 38, 39
mosaics **4:** 13, 14, 21; **5:** 33
mud **4:** 11
muskets **2:** 45

N

nail manufacture **2:** 56
nail polish **1:** 46
native copper **2:** 37
native gold **2:** 4, 36
native metals **2:** 4, 36
natural adhesives **3:** 46, 51, 53, 54; **6:** 48-49
natural dyes **6:** 7, 11-13
natural fibers **1:** 13; **6:** 7, 17, 18, 20, 21, 24; **7:** 7, 9, 10, 12, 14, 19-30, 31, 32, 34, 36, 38, 44, 46
natural gas **1:** 17, 28; **9:** 48
natural polymers **1:** 6, 7, 8-9; **7:** 10-12, 14
natural resins **3:** 10, 13, 14, 20, 23, 27, 46, 52, 54, 56; **6:** 37
natural rubber **1:** 7, 8-9, 12, 13, 42
natural varnishes **6:** 37
neon **9:** 18, 54, 57
neoprene **1:** 42; **6:** 52
nets **7:** 22, 44, 49
neutrons **2:** 6
newspaper, newsprint papers **3:** 46, 52, 56
nickel **2:** 9, 24, 26, 30; **4:** 47, 48; **5:** 11
nitric oxide **9:** 30

nitrogen cycle **9:** 38
nitrogen dioxide **9:** 13, 19, 21, 39, 40
nitrogen, nitrogen gas **1:** 21; **9:** 18, 36, 37-42
nitrogen oxides (Nox) **9:** 13, 18, 19, 21, 30, 37, 38, 39, 40, 46
nitrous oxide **9:** 18
noble gases **9:** 53-57
nonflammable gases **9:** 54
noniron plastics **1:** 45, 47
nonmetals **2:** 6, 8; **5:** 18
nonstick plastics **1:** 10, 41
Nox. *See* nitrogen oxides
nucleating agent **5:** 14
nylon **1:** 13, 48-49, 50; **6:** 8, 20; **7:** 10, 14, 30, 31, 32–33, 34, 35, 36, 37, 47-51, 52, 57

O

oak **3:** 5, 17, 18, 19, 29
obsidian **5:** 7
oceans, ocean water **8:** 4, 6, 37
oil **8:** 28, 32
oil paint, oil-based paints **6:** 29, 35
oils **3:** 10; **9:** 45, 48, 49, 54. *See also* crude oil
olefin, olefin fibers **7:** 36, 52
opacity in materials **1:** 24, 30, 33; **3:** 51, 54; **5:** 7, 14
open-pit mining **2:** 5
optic fiber casings **1:** 12
optic fibers, optical fibers, optical glass fibers **1:** 46, 47; **7:** 55
optical properties of glass **5:** 20
optical structures **4:** 44
option **4:** 44, 46, 50
ores **2:** 5, 9, 37, 38
oriented strand board **3:** 42, 44
Orlon® **1:** 39; **7:** 45
osmosis **8:** 40-41
Otis, Elisha **2:** 57
outer bark **3:** 12
oven glass **5:** 9
ovenware **5:** 12
oxide film, oxide coat **2:** 10, 11, 29, 30, 32
oxidizing agent **8:** 7, 53
oxygen **1:** 13, 35, 37, 40, 53, 54, 55, 57; **2:** 4, 6, 10, 38, 52; **4:** 6, 7, 8, 14, 27, 53; **8:** 4, 7, 8, 9, 10, 14, 37, 42, 46, 53, 55-56; **9:** 10, 11, 12, 18, 19, 20, 21, 36, 38, 39, 41, 43-45, 47, 48, 51, 54, 55
oxygen cycle **9:** 43
ozone **1:** 29, 57; **9:** 19, 20, 21, 44

P

packaging material **1:** 21, 22, 29, 30, 32, 33, 34, 37, 57; **3:** 46, 51, 57
pad-dry dyeing **6:** 22, 23
painting metals **2:** 28, 29, 33
painting wood **3:** 8, 41
paints **1:** 37, 41, 45, 53p; **6:** 4-16, 27-40
palladium **2:** 26; **4:** 46
PAN. *See* polyacrylonitrile
panning **2:** 4
paper **1:** 22, 23, 37, 44, 46; **3:** 4, 11, 34, 46-57; **6:** 9; **7:** 8, 19, 20, 41; **8:** 26, 29
papermaking **3:** 50-54
paper stock **3:** 54
paper towels **3:** 56
paper weight **3:** 46

papier-mâché **6:** 42
papyrus **3:** 46, 47; **6:** 42
Parkesine **1:** 46
particleboard **1:** 44; **3:** 44
paste, flour-based **6:** 42
patina **2:** 28
PC. *See* polycarbonate
PE. *See* polyethylene
periodic table **2:** 8, 50
permanent hardness **8:** 55
permanent magnets **2:** 10
permanent-press fabrics **7:** 16-17, 44. *See also* durable- and stay-pressed fabrics
Perspex® **1:** 38, 39
PET or PETE. *See* polyethylene terephthalate
petrochemicals **1:** 12; **7:** 8
petroleum, petroleum products **1:** 12; **7:** 12, 31, 52
phenolic varnishes **6:** 37
phenols, phenolic resin **1:** 21, 43, 44
phlogiston **9:** 51
Phoenicians **5:** 32
phosphoric acid **5:** 17
phosphors **4:** 51, 52
photochemical smog **9:** 40
photochromic glasses **5:** 22
photosynthesis **9:** 21, 43, 48
piezoelectrics **4:** 47-48
pigments **1:** 16, 24, 30, 37, 53; **3:** 54; **4:** 51; **6:** 6-10, 11, 27, 29, 40; **7:** 38
Pilkington, Alastair **5:** 49
pine **3:** 16, 23, 27
pistols **2:** 45
pistons **8:** 21, 22
pith **3:** 13
planks **3:** 34, 36, 37, 39
plaster **4:** 18, 34
plaster of Paris **4:** 34
plastering **4:** 34
plastic bags **1:** 4, 10, 13, 18, 22, 28, 29
plastic bottles **1:** 4, 15, 19, 20, 24, 25, 26, 29, 30, 31, 32, 50, 51
plastic change **2:** 22, 35
plastic film **1:** 7, 18, 29, 37, 46, 47
plasticity **1:** 4
plasticity in ceramics **4:** 8, 28, 29
plasticity in glass **5:** 23
plasticity in wood **3:** 19
plasticizers **1:** 15, 16, 21; **7:** 17
plastic metal **6:** 51
plastics **1:** 4 AND THROUGHOUT; **2:** 4, 12, 14, 33; **3:** 6; **4:** 43, 49, 56; **5:** 26; **6:** 41, 43, 49; **7:** 8, 32; **9:** 41, 50
plastic sheet **1:** 6, 7, 11, 18, 20, 22, 23, 37, 38, 42, 44, 47, 50
plastic wood **6:** 51
plate glass **5:** 41, 49
plating **2:** 30, 32
platinum **2:** 10, 11, 21; **4:** 43, 57; **8:** 55
pleats **7:** 16, 17, 44
Plexiglas® **1:** 38
pliable properties of wood **3:** 19, 22
plows, plowshares **2:** 44, 46
plumbing **2:** 43
plutonium oxides **4:** 54
plywood **1:** 22, 44; **3:** 24, 42, 43
PMMA. *See* polymethyl methacrylate
pneumatic devices **9:** 29-31
pneumatic trough **9:** 10
polar solvent **8:** 43
polarity in water **8:** 9, 10, 11
poles **3:** 33
polish **3:** 8
polishing **5:** 24, 30, 49, 50, 51
pollution **8:** 51, 57. *See also* air pollution
pollution control **2:** 11
polyacrylonitrile (PAN) **7:** 45
polyamides **1:** 48; **7:** 47, 49
polycarbonate (PC) **1:** 13, 52, 53
polychloroethylene **1:** 10
polyester **6:** 21
polyester fiber **1:** 13, 47; **7:** 10, 14, 17, 18, 31, 32, 33, 34, 36, 42-44, 46, 49, 50, 51, 54
polyethers **1:** 13, 22, 50-54
polyethylene (PE) **1:** 4, 10, 11, 20, 21, 22, 26, 27, 28-30, 31, 32; **7:** 33, 52; **8:** 28
polyethylene terephthalate (PETE or PET) **1:** 20, 24, 25, 26, 50-51; **6:** 21; **7:** 32, 37, 42
polyisoprene **1:** 8
polymer industry **1:** 8
polymerization **1:** 10; **7:** 10, 14, 15, 49
polymer membrane **8:** 41
polymers **1:** 6, 7, 10, 13, 14, 15, 16, 27, 28, 37, 38, 41; **3:** 10; **6:** 17, 28, 43, 49; **7:** 9, 10-14, 31, 32, 33
polymethyl methacrylate (PMMA) **1:** 40-41
polypropylene (PP) **1:** 11, 20, 26, 27, 31-33; **7:** 52
polypropylene fibers **7:** 33, 38, 52
polystyrene (PS) **1:** 10, 14, 20, 21, 23, 24, 26, 33-34, 47, 54; **6:** 57
polytetrafluoroethylene (PTFE) **1:** 10, 41
polyurethane adhesives **6:** 50
polyurethane fibers **7:** 52
polyurethanes **1:** 21, 56-57
polyurethane varnishes **6:** 37
polyvinyl acetate (PVA, PVAc) **1:** 37; **6:** 54
polyvinyl acetate (PVA) adhesive **6:** 54-55, 57
polyvinyl acetate (PVA) glue **1:** 37
polyvinyl chloride (PVC) **1:** 10, 13, 14, 15, 16, 20, 21, 25, 26, 35, 36, 37. *See also* vinyl
polyvinylidene (PVDC) **1:** 36, 37
poplar **3:** 17
porcelain **2:** 26, 57; **4:** 22, 25-26, 52, 56
porcelain enamel **4:** 23; **5:** 14
pores **7:** 30
porous ceramics **4:** 18, 30, 31, 40, 55
Portland cement **4:** 35, 37, 38
Portland cement plant **4:** 36-37
Post-it® Notes **6:** 54
posts **3:** 33
potash **5:** 8, 9
potassium **2:** 5, 8, 10
potato glue **6:** 49
potential energy **8:** 35
pottery **4:** 4, 17, 31
powder coatings **6:** 40
powder forming **2:** 13, 21
powder glass **5:** 52
powder paints **6:** 12, 13
powders **4:** 9, 34, 35, 37, 38, 43-44, 46, 48, 49, 50, 51, 52, 55
PP. *See* polypropylene
precipitation **8:** 55, 57
preservatives **3:** 30, 33, 40, 41; **6:** 36
preserving wood **3:** 30, 40-41
pressing **2:** 20
pressure **9:** 5, 8, 12, 13
pressure cooker **8:** 21
pressure of a gas **9:** 8, 9, 14, 15. *See also* air pressure
pressure-sensitive adhesives (PSAs) **6:** 54
pressure-treated wood **3:** 33, 40
primary colors **6:** 4
primers **6:** 28, 30, 33
Prince Rupert's Drop **5:** 10
properties of gases **9:** 12-17
properties of wood **3:** 19-29
propylene **1:** 11, 28
protective clothing **1:** 14, 48
protective coatings **6:** 27-40
proteins **6:** 17, 48, 49; **7:** 4, 10, 26, 28
protons **2:** 6
PS. *See* polystyrene
PSAs. *See* pressure-sensitive adhesives
PTFE. *See* polytetrafluoroethylene
pugging **4:** 28
pulp fibers **3:** 53
pulp, pulp production **3:** 32, 45, 46, 48, 51-54, 56
pumping engine **8:** 21
pumps **9:** 5, 6, 8, 28
pure liquids **8:** 49
pure water **8:** 6, 49
PVA adhesive **6:** 54-55, 57
PVA glue **1:** 37
PVA, PVAc. *See* polyvinyl acetate
PVC. *See* polyvinyl chloride
PVDC. *See* polyvinylidene
Pyrex® **5:** 12, 13

Q

quartzite **5:** 9
quenching **2:** 41

R

radiation **9:** 21, 22, 27
radiators **9:** 26, 27
radioactive water **8:** 14, 15
radiometer **9:** 14
radon **9:** 54, 56
raffia **7:** 19
rags, rag fibers **3:** 49
railroads, railroad stations and tracks **2:** 17, 18, 48, 49, 54
rain, rainwater **8:** 5, 57
rare earths **4:** 51
Ravenscroft, George **5:** 37
rayon **1:** 47, 48, 51; **3:** 50
rayon fiber **7:** 10, 12, 13, 17, 24, 31, 36, 37, 39-41, 57
rays **3:** 12, 14
reactive **9:** 43
reactive dyes **7:** 30
reactivity of metals **2:** 10-11
reactivity of water **8:** 6, 16, 53, 54
reactivity series **2:** 10; **8:** 54
ready-mixed concrete **4:** 39
recycling **1:** 12, 20, 23-26, 51; **3:** 56-57; **4:** 16; **5:** 3, 6, 41, 42
red oak **3:** 18
reducing agent **8:** 7
redwood **3:** 11, 13, 16
refiners **3:** 53
reflective paints **6:** 39
refraction in glass **5:** 20
refractive index of glass **5:** 21, 37, 55, 56

refractory bricks **4**: 31, 32, 33
refractory, refractory materials **4**: 6, 24, 31, 32-33
refrigerants **8**: 33; **9**: 41, 50
regenerated fibers **7**: 12, 31
reinforced concrete **4**: 40
reinforced fiber **4**: 10
reinforcers **1**: 15, 16; **7**: 57
reinforcing plastics **1**: 15, 16, 23, 44
repositionable adhesives **6**: 54
resin enamel **2**: 33; **6**: 38
Resin Identification Code **1**: 25, 26
resins **1**: 6, 11, 16, 22, 44, 53; **2**: 33; **4**: 43, 55, 56; **6**: 27, 37; **7**: 53, 54, 56, 57. *See also* natural resins and synthetic resins
respiration **9**: 12, 43, 48
respositionable adhesives **6**: 54
rifles **2**: 44, 45
rifling **2**: 45
rising damp **8**: 37
rivets **2**: 43, 52
road materials **4**: 41
Robert, Nicolas-Louis **3**: 46
rocks **8**: 4, 5, 6, 7
rocks and metals **2**: 4, 5, 36, 37, 38, 40, 43, 46, 50
rod glass **5**: 53
rolled glass **5**: 10
rolling **2**: 13, 17, 18, 23
rolling mill **2**: 18, 49
rolls of paper **3**: 51
Roman armor **2**: 40, 43
Romans **2**: 38, 40, 41, 42, 43, 55; **4**: 13, 55; **5**: 34, 38, 39, 49; **9**: 25
roof tiles **1**: 10, 18, 21
rope **7**: 19, 20, 22, 44, 48, 49
rosin **3**: 53
rotary saws **3**: 37
rough sawing **3**: 34-36
rubber **1**: 6, 7, 8, 9, 12, 13, 15, 21, 29, 42, 43, 56; **6**: 9, 49, 52; **7**: 37
rubber tree **1**: 8
ruby, synthetic **4**: 52
rugs **6**: 14; **7**: 27
rust **2**: 11, 27, 28, 29, 30; **8**: 53
rust-preventative surface coatings **6**: 28, 29, 30, 33
ruthenium dioxide **4**: 52

S

sacks, sacking **7**: 11, 20, 21
saffron **6**: 13
salt, salts **8**: 4, 5, 6, 7, 19, 40, 41, 42, 43, 44, 45, 46, 47, 48, 50, 55
sand **4**: 10, 12, 13, 15, 16, 17, 22, 29, 33, 36, 38, 39; **5**: 4, 8, 29
sap **3**: 14, 22, 47
sapphire **4**: 50
sapwood **3**: 10, 12, 13, 14
satin paint **6**: 34
saturated air **8**: 18
saturated solutions **8**: 44
sawdust **3**: 34
sawmill **3**: 23, 31, 34-35
sawn timber **3**: 8, 23, 36, 37
sculpting wood **3**: 8, 9
sealants **1**: 55; **6**: 43, 50, 56
seawater **8**: 7, 9, 19, 41, 42, 47, 50
selenium oxide **5**: 11
semiconductors **5**: 15
semigloss paint **6**: 34

semimetals **2**: 8
semipermeable membranes **8**: 40, 41
sensors **4**: 53
sewage **8**: 6, 41, 51
shakes **3**: 20, 26
shales **4**: 15, 28, 29, 30, 38
shaped glass **5**: 54
sheet glass **5**: 10
sheet-metal **2**: 13, 18, 20
shellac **1**: 6
shingles **3**: 8
shot **2**: 45
siding **3**: 7, 22
Siemens, Friedrich **2**: 47
silica **4**: 15, 38, 46, 57; **5**: 8
silica glasses **5**: 8, 9, 52
silicon **1**: 27, 43, 55; **4**: 14, 36, 37
silicon carbide **4**: 57
silicon chips **4**: 4, 6, 42, 43; **9**: 53
silicon dioxide **4**: 5, 38; **5**: 8
silicone-based adhesives and sealants **1**: 57, 55; **6**: 50, 51, 56-57
silk **1**: 6; **6**: 17; **7**: 4, 6, 10, 19, 21, 28-29; **8**: 29
silk cocoons **6**: 41; **7**: 28
silk substitute **7**: 46
silkworm **6**: 41; **7**: 4, 28
silver **2**: 4, 9, 10, 11, 25, 26, 36, 37, 39, 40, 43; **4**: 46; **8**: 55
silver halide **5**: 22
silver oxide **5**: 11
sinter, sintering **2**: 21; **4**: 9, 44
sisal, sisal fibers **3**: 47; **7**: 19
sizing **3**: 51, 53
skateboard wheels **1**: 56, 57
skein **7**: 22
skyscrapers **2**: 56, 57
slag **2**: 24, 40, 41
slip casting **4**: 17
smell **9**: 17
smelting **2**: 38
soap **8**: 30-31, 46, 55
soda **5**: 8, 9, 10, 17, 18, 22, 29, 38
soda-lime glass **5**: 8, 11, 12, 13, 19, 21, 23, 37, 38, 42, 48
sodium **2**: 5, 7, 10
sodium carbonate **5**: 9
sodium nitrate **5**: 11
sodium oxide **5**: 9
soft-mud process **4**: 28
softwoods, softwood forests **3**: 16, 17, 30, 48, 50
solar cells **5**: 52
solder **2**: 25
solidification **8**: 16
solids **5**: 5; **8**: 4, 5, 16, 17, 24; **9**: 5, 12
solubility of substances in water **8**: 45
solutes **8**: 41, 42
solution **8**: 6, 19, 32, 40, 42, 44
solvay process **5**: 38
solvents **1**: 39, 53; **6**: 27, 33, 34, 35, 37, 38, 40, 52, 54, 57; **8**: 6, 10, 41, 42, 43
sound and wood **3**: 8, 29-30
sound insulation **3**: 8, 29, 30
sound in water **8**: 39
sound-proofing **3**: 29
Space Shuttle **4**: 42; **5**: 52; **7**: 57
space suits **7**: 50-51
spandex **1**: 57; **7**: 36, 52
special fibers **7**: 53-57
speciality plastics **1**: 13

spectrum **5**: 20
spinneret **7**: 32, 34, 35, 36, 37, 41, 42, 45, 46, 47
spinning **1**: 7, 25; **7**: 7, 9, 21, 22, 34-36, 37, 40, 41
spinning bobbins **7**: 21
spinning wheels **7**: 21
springwood **3**: 14
spruce **3**: 16
stabilizers **1**: 15, 16; **5**: 8, 9, 13, 16
stained glass **5**: 34
stainless steel **2**: 19, 24, 27, 31, 32, 34
stains, paint **6**: 32, 34, 36
stalactite **8**: 57
stannite **2**: 37
staple **7**: 21, 25, 40
starch glues **3**: 43; **6**: 49
states of matter **5**: 5; **8**: 16
states of water **8**: 16
static electricity buildup **7**: 43, 52
Statue of Liberty **2**: 19, 20
stay-pressed fabrics **1**: 51. *See also* durable- and permanent-press fabrics
stealth technology **4**: 49
steam **8**: 16, 19, 20, 21
steam-driven engines **2**: 47, 49
steam engines **8**: 21-23
steam heating **3**: 22, 36, 43
steam turbines **8**: 23, 34
steel **1**: 7, 13, 15, 48; **2**: 10, 11, 13, 17, 18, 19, 22, 23, 24, 27, 28, 29, 30, 31, 32, 34, 39, 41, 42, 43, 45, 46, 47, 49, 50, 51, 54, 56, 57
sterling silver **2**: 11, 26
stiff-mud process **4**: 28
stone **4**: 4, 12, 26, 28, 39, 41
Stone Age **5**: 7
Stone Age ax **4**: 5
stoneware **4**: 22, 24, 25
strand **7**: 4, 20, 21, 28
stratosphere **9**: 20
straw **3**: 49
strength of metal alloys **2**: 23
strength of wood **3**: 24-26
strengthening glass **5**: 24-27
strengthening, strengthening agents in paper **3**: 48, 49, 54
stretching fibers **7**: 36
strontium carbonate **5**: 9
studding **3**: 38
styrene **1**: 10
styrene-butadiene rubber **1**: 42
styrofoam **1**: 4, 14, 33; **6**: 57
sublimation **8**: 16, 17
subtractive colors **6**: 4
suction pump **9**: 5, 6
sugarcane **3**: 49
suits of armor **2**: 43, 44
sulfur **1**: 13, 27, 29, 43
sulfur dioxide **9**: 19, 46-47
summerwood **3**: 14
super glue **1**: 40, 41; **6**: 54
superconductivity in metals **2**: 9
superconductors **4**: 8, 45
superheated water **8**: 20, 54
surface coating glass **5**: 22
surface coatings **1**: 45, 56; **6**: 4-40
surface tension **8**: 11, 14, 25-26, 28, 37
surfactants **8**: 29
suspensions **8**: 6
sweaters **7**: 27, 44

swords 2: 36, 40, 41, 42, 43, 44
synthetic adhesives 3: 43, 44; 6: 43, 49-50
synthetic ceramics 4: 48
synthetic dye industry 6: 15
synthetic dyes 6: 7, 10, 14, 15, 26; 7: 38
synthetic fibers 1: 7, 13, 48, 50; 3: 50; 7: 7, 12, 14, 18, 24, 31, 38
synthetic polymers 1: 6, 7; 7: 14
synthetic resins 3: 43, 44
synthetic rubber 1: 6, 7, 13, 42
synthetics 1: 7

T
tableware 4: 16, 24, 25
tangled 7: 21
tannins 3: 10
tarmacadam 4: 41
tarnishing 2: 10, 11; 5: 23
teak 3: 17, 19
Teflon® 1: 10, 41; 4: 44
tektites 5: 7
tempering metals 2: 23, 41
tempering, tempered glass 5: 25, 26
temporarily hard water 8: 55
tensile glass temperature 7: 17
tensile strength 7: 7
tension weakness in ceramics 4: 8
terra cotta 4: 31
Terylene® 1: 50; 7: 33, 42
tetrafluoroethylene 1: 10
thermal capacity 8: 34, 36. *See also* heat capacity
thermal properties of glass 5: 18
thermals 9: 9
thermistors 4: 53
thermometers 5: 12, 53
thermoplastic adhesives 6: 50
thermoplastic fibers 7: 44
thermoplastic resins 1: 11
thermoplastics 1: 10, 11, 12, 13, 15, 20, 24, 31, 35, 43
thermosets, thermosetting plastics 1: 11, 12, 13, 20, 22, 23, 24, 43, 44, 46, 57; 6: 50; 7: 44
thermosphere 9: 20
thread 7: 4, 22, 44, 49
tie dyeing 6: 19
tiles, ceramic tiles 4: 10, 16, 17, 21, 23, 24, 25, 26, 31, 42
timber 3: 4, 34, 36, 38, 39
tin 2: 8, 10, 24, 25, 26, 30, 37, 38, 40
tin ore 2: 38
tin oxide 4: 53
tin plating 2: 30; 8: 54
tinting glass 5: 21
tin-vanadium oxide 4: 51
tire cord 7: 37, 41, 44, 49
tires 1: 8, 42, 51; 9: 28, 29
titanium 2: 22, 50, 51, 54
titanium dioxide 4: 46
toilet tissue 3: 54
top coat 6: 28, 30, 31, 34
tortoiseshell 1: 46
toughened glass 5: 25
toxic fumes or smoke 1: 14, 25
transistor 4: 6, 45
transition metals 2: 8; 4: 51
translucent plastics 1: 12, 13, 30, 53
transparency in materials 1: 4, 12, 21, 24, 26, 28, 30, 33, 34, 37, 38, 40, 52; 4: 20, 50, 53; 5: 4, 6, 15, 19; 6: 27, 37, 38, 55

tree rings *See* growth rings
tree trunks 3: 6, 11, 12, 13, 14, 15, 16, 23, 27, 32, 33
Trevira® 7: 42
triacetate 7: 36
Tricel® 1: 47; 7: 46
tritium 8: 14
troposphere 9: 19, 20
trusses 2: 54, 55
tube glass 5: 53
tube metal 2: 19, 44
tumblers 5: 48
tungsten 2: 9, 21, 53
tungsten carbide 4: 57
tunnel kilns 4: 19, 25, 28, 30, 31
turpentine 6: 37
tweeds 7: 27
twenty-four-carat gold 2: 26
twine 7: 11, 22

U
unbleached paper 3: 56
undercoat 6: 28, 30, 31, 33
universal solvent 8: 43
unreactive metals 2: 4, 8, 11
uPVC. *See* polyvinyl chloride
uranium 5: 11
uranium oxides 4: 54
urea 1: 44
urethane 1: 53
utility poles 3: 28

V
V. *See* vinyl and polyvinyl chloride
vacuum 9: 6, 35, 55
vacuum forming 1: 19, 20
vacuum pump 9: 8, 11, 13
valency forces 6: 45
valve 9: 6, 7, 28, 31, 39
vapor 8: 4. *See also* water vapor
vaporize, vaporization 8: 16
varnishes 1: 11; 6: 37, 38
vat dyeing 6: 20-21
veneers 3: 9, 18, 42, 43; 6: 42
Venetian glassmakers 5: 36
vinyl (V) 1: 26, 28, 34-38. *See also* polyvinyl chloride
vinyl acetate 1: 39; 7: 45
vinyl chloride 1: 10; 7: 45
vinyl emulsion 6: 34
vinyl varnishes 6: 37
vinyl wallpaper 6: 47
viscose fiber 1: 47, 50; 6: 20; 7: 36, 39, 40, 41
viscose process 7: 36, 39-41
viscosity of gases 9: 13, 15
viscosity of water 8: 14, 32, 39
vitreous china 4: 20
vitreous enamel, vitreous enameling 4: 23; 5: 13, 14; 5: 13, 14
vitrify, vitrification 4: 19-20, 22, 25, 27, 28

W
wallboards 4: 34
wallpaper adhesive 6: 47
warping 3: 19, 24
wash and wear fabrics 7: 44
waste paper 3: 56, 57
water 7: 7, 10, 17, 18; 9: 4, 5, 16, 21, 22, 27, 30, 46, 47, 48, 53, 54; 8: 4 AND THROUGHOUT
water-based adhesives 6: 49, 55, 57

water-based paints 6: 29, 34-35, 36
water cycle 8: 4-6
water heaters 8: 33, 38
water, influence on properties of wood 3: 20-24, 28
water in papermaking 3: 50-51
water molecules 8: 8-13, 44
waterproof fibers 7: 8, 18, 26, 48
waterproofing 8: 28-29
waterproof or watertight ceramics 4: 9, 10, 11, 19, 20, 21, 22, 23, 25, 29
water softeners 8: 55
water vapor 8: 4, 6, 16, 17, 19, 20, 49; 9: 3, 9, 16, 19, 21, 36, 49, 51-53
Watt, James 2: 56
waxes 3: 10
wear resistance of metal alloys 2: 23
weaving 7: 7, 8, 22, 23
web of paper 3: 51
welding 1: 18, 22, 29, 37; 2: 27, 52
wet felting 3: 45
wet spinning 7: 36, 40
wetting 6: 46-47
wetting agents 8: 28-29
wet water 8: 37
white glass 5: 11, 36
white glue 6: 54
whitewares 4: 16, 22-26, 29, 30, 33
windows and window glass 7, 10, 42, 46, 49, 52
windshields 5: 21, 23, 26, 27, 54
winning 4: 28
wire 2: 19, 31, 53
wire-reinforced glass 5: 26
wood 6: 13; 1: 22, 37, 44, 45; 2: 12, 15, 36, 40, 44, 46, 47, 48, 55; 3: 4 AND THROUGHOUT; 5: 7
wood cells 3: 10. *See also* cells
wood chips 7: 12, 38
wooden tiles 3: 8
wood products in building 3: 5, 7, 8, 16, 23, 26, 28, 34, 44
wood pulp processing 7: 31
wool 1: 13, 39, 51; 3: 51; 6: 14, 17; 7: 6, 10, 19, 21, 26, 43, 45
worsteds 7: 27
wrought iron 2: 40, 41, 44, 49, 55

X
xenon 9: 18, 54, 56

Y
yarn 7: 22, 25, 28
yew 3: 16, 17
yttrium vanadate 4: 52

Z
Zachariasen, W. H. 5: 39
zinc 2: 3, 6, 10, 11, 13, 16, 24, 25, 26, 27, 30, 31, 41
zinc coating or plating 2: 3, 6, 11, 13, 30, 31
zinc oxide 4: 56; 5: 9
zircon 4: 52
zirconia 4: 4, 53
zirconium dioxide. *See* zirconia
zirconium oxide 5: 9
zirconium silicate. *See* zircon
zirconium–vanadium oxide 4: 51